*And now let's move into a time
of nonsense ...*

And now let's move into a time of nonsense ...

WHY WORSHIP SONGS ARE FAILING THE CHURCH

Nick Page

Copyright © 2004 Nick Page

10 09 08 07 06 05 04   8 7 6 5 4 3 2 1

First published in 2004 by Authentic Media
9 Holdom Avenue, Bletchley, Milton Keynes, MK1 1QR, UK
and PO Box 1047, Waynesboro, GA 30830-2047
www.paternoster-publishing.com

The right of Nick Page to be identified as the author
of this work has been asserted by him in accordance with the
Copyright, Designs and Patents Act 1988.

British Library Cataloguing in Publication Data
A catalogue record for this book is available from the British Library

ISBN 1-85078-584-8

Cover design by Peter Barnsley
Print Management by Adare Carwin
Typeset by Waverley Typesetters, Galashiels

DEDICATION:

To Little Maisie, with the fervent hope that one day she will recover the use of the lower limb on the right hand side of her body ...

About the Author

Nick Page is a writer, information designer, creative consultant and the author of over twenty books, including *The Tabloid Bible, The Bible Book* and *Church Invisible*. He and his family live in Eynsham, Oxfordshire.

Contents

Introduction: or
Two-edged swords in Luton   1

How we got here: or
A brief history of worship music   9

But they're only words: or
Why worship matters   22

From poet to pop star: or
How we got into this mess   36

As long as you're sincere: or
The importance of technique   52

Cracking the code: or
The problem of language   84

Conclusion: or
Where do we go from here?   111

Appendix 1: Some technical stuff   117

Appendix 2: Literary patterns   119

Appendix 3: Kevin's songs   122

Kevin Molecule
27a Cinderpile Crescent
Stoke Poges

Mr Dave Davey
Songs of Dwellingness Ministries
Briglimpton
SUSSEX

Dear Mr Davey,

I am an anointed worship leader in my
church – the Stoke Poges Strict Tabernacle
– and I notice that you are responsible for
collecting and publishing worship songs,
both in your Songs of Dwellingness Books
and for the annual Summer Reaping
conferences.

Anyway, for some time now I have been
sharing my anointing with my church in the
form of worship songs and my pastor, Gerald
Freely, suggested I send one to you for
possible inclusion in your collections or
on one of your 'Lord Save Us!' CDs. You will
find the song on the enclosed CD as performed
by our worship band.

For your further information these are the
lyrics.

Jesus, Jesus, Jesus
We glorify the Lamb once slain
Jesus, Jesus, Jesus
We enter into the land all over again.
Build a great big throne with our worship,
Help us live in resurrection power;

And you will reign
Like a bride ordained,
For our anointed consummating hour.

Repeat
Jesus, Jesus, Jesus, etc.

I hope this is of interest to you. Any
advice, criticism gratefully received,
although you ought to be aware that I have
been anointed so any criticism of me will,
technically, be criticising God.

With deep humility,

Kevin Molecule
Worship Leader

Introduction: or
Two-edged swords in Luton

Flashback. It's some time in the early 1990s and I'm attending a friend's wedding in Luton. The church is packed and because so many of the congregation are non-Christians, the minister is making a special effort to help them feel involved. He's explaining every step of the service in simple, clear language and the amazing thing is that they're with him all the way. You can see it on their faces. In all the weddings they must have attended – including maybe their own – no one has ever explained it to them. For the first time, it's like they understand what's going on in church.

And then we start singing.

And all that hopeful comprehension drains away, lost in a sea of quasi-biblical imagery and incomprehensible language. The couple getting married had included a time of worship, they told me afterwards, to show their non-Christian families that Christian music could be contemporary and relevant. They may have been right about the music; maybe we showed them that day that Christians could play a decent tune with the best of them. But as we sang songs about two-edged swords and anointing oil and lots and lots of sheep, we also showed them that, when it comes to song lyrics, Christians speak an entirely different language.

As I stood there, looking at the non-Christians while they stumbled through the lyrics or exchanged baffled, uncomprehending looks with each other, I suddenly realised one blinding, staggering fact: I didn't understand the words either.

I'd been a Christian for years. I'd taken part in big Christian events, worked for a major Christian charity; I'd paid my dues. And I didn't understand a word I was singing.

Great tunes, shame about the words

Recent decades have seen an explosion of worship song writing. Each year brings new worship songs, CDs and song books to be rapidly devoured by a hungry church.

But now, as much as ever, I feel like those folk at the wedding. When I look at the words on my service sheet every Sunday morning they don't seem to connect with me. Either they're so banal as to be risible, or they're filled with more biblical imagery than any other book except, well, the Bible. They often don't scan very well; they frequently attempt rhymes that you could only call 'optimistic'; they're often little more than a collection of Bible verses, ripped out of context and shoe-horned into a lyric.

Why is this? Why, when the tunes are often so good, are the lyrics frequently so bad? Why are we content to stand there in church and sing stuff that really doesn't make any sense?

All right. I'm overstating the case. But, in the ten years or so since my experience on the road to Luton, I have talked to a great many people about the quality – or lack of it – of the words that we sing each week. And I wasn't alone. I've met scores of people who are as frustrated as I am. I've talked to many well-known and well-respected Christian leaders who share my opinions. A good friend told me he preferred playing in the worship band because 'at least then I don't have to sing the things'.

But nothing seemed to happen about it. The leaders still stood on the platforms at major events and happily sang along. The words continue to churn out by their millions.

We're supposed to love God with our heart and soul and mind, but, where worship songs are concerned, we settle for two out of three, putting our mind on pause while we sing incomprehensible songs with archaic imagery and repetitive themes.

It's as if we're all shrugging our shoulders and saying 'nothing can be done'.

Well, this book is an attempt to do something about it.

'What do you know?'

This book originated as an article in *Christianity* magazine.[1] I wrote it more as a kind of therapy exercise; I mean you can only go on singing these things for so long. What surprised me was the depth of response. The editor told me that the article had generated more feedback than anything they'd published in the past seven years.

Many of the responses were in agreement, many were in complete disagreement. Some people called me 'Victor Meldrew'. Most either misquoted the article or misunderstood what I was saying. Some people said to me that I shouldn't have had the temerity to write about worship songs if I didn't write any myself. This is a strong point, although not, I think, a valid one. As Dr Johnson said, you don't have to be a carpenter to know when a table is badly made.[2]

---

[1] 'We need some new songs', *Christianity and Renewal*, August 2003.

[2] He actually said, 'You may abuse a tragedy though you cannot write one. You may scold a carpenter who has made you a bad table, though you cannot make a table. It is not your trade to make tables.' James

Although I play occasionally in my church worship group, I don't have any formal musical training beyond Grade 5 Clarinet. And I think I only passed that because the examiner was quite obviously sorry for me.

What I do know about is words. I've studied poetry and writers for most of my life. I may not know much about leading corporate worship, but I know when a line just doesn't work.

But anyway, all this misses the point. The point is that I don't want this book to tear down but to build up. I'm really just trying to address the need for people to care about the words they sing and the words they write. Things, as the saying goes, could be better. That's all this book is about.

So, if I occasionally go over the top, I apologise. Look on it as the insane ramblings of the Victor Meldrew of the Christian world.

I love you all really ...

Let me make one thing clear at the start: I admire and respect those who write our worship songs, and, unlike so many critics of the modern worship song, I don't want to go back to hymns.[3] Those who call for a return to the good old days of hymn-singing generally forget that the hymns which we use regularly are just a tiny fraction of the hymns which were written. The cream, over the centuries, has risen to the surface, but believe me, beneath that cream lies an ocean of curdled milk. Wesley was capable of writing great hymns – but he also wrote many moderate hymns, and not a few complete clunkers.

Boswell, *Life of Samuel Johnson* (London: George Allen & Unwin, 1924) I, p. 251. I just thought my version was pithier!

[3] Technically that's making two things clear at the start, but who's counting?

In any case, I'm not sure that there's much difference between a hymn and a worship song, except for the era in which they were written. Hymns tend to have a formal structure and to rhyme; worship songs are freer and are in blank verse. But is 'Make way, make way'[4] a worship song or a hymn? It has verses, rhymes, yet its style is unmistakably that of the modern worship song. Fundamentally I think that both worship songs and hymns share a common heritage and a common purpose. I hope to show in this book that the people who wrote the first modern hymns were only trying to do what worship song writers are trying to do today.

No, I like worship songs. If I didn't like them I wouldn't get so annoyed about them. If I didn't feel they were worth arguing over I'd go and do something else with my time. I believe that the modern worship song is an immensely powerful vehicle for worship, and a major factor in encouraging, sustaining and strengthening the spiritual lives of many millions of Christians around the world.

And I know that the people who write these songs do so from the best of motives: to bring people closer to God. They are gifted people, writing from a desire to see people deepen their relationship with God. So I don't want to knock the people writing them, or to single anyone out for individual criticism. I don't want people to stop writing worship songs: I just want them to write *better*.

What I've tried to do in this book is look at the words of the songs. I want to look at what worship is, where the songs we sing come from and how we can help people to worship more effectively, more deeply and with more personal relevance. Inevitably that means citing specific examples, but for the most part, you won't find

---

[4] Graham Kendrick, SOF 384, 1986.

direct quotes from songs in this book. This is for two main reasons. Firstly, believe it or not, I am trying to be positive and I don't want to be seen to be 'picking' on individuals. Secondly, and perhaps more fundamentally, most publishers refused me permission to quote from the songs unless I was saying something nice about them! I can't say I entirely blame them, given the title of the book, but even so, it was a bit of a surprise to find such a reaction.

Mostly, the publishers argued that these songs were written from the best of motives, or that they were very precious to the writer and so it was unfair to criticise them. I have to say that I think this is nonsense. I will deal with the question of motive later, but right at the start I'd like to say that if you want people to sing your songs, you'd better be prepared for them to question them. Just because your motives are good, that doesn't mean your songs are good. A pure heart is no guarantee of genius. I believe passionately that we have a right to criticise the content, the style, the structure of anything intended for public consumption – whether we're talking about a sermon or a soap opera. If you want people to sing your songs, you have to be prepared to allow the words to be criticised.

So there are a few times when I refer to individual songs or to different examples. If I didn't do this, I felt I would be accused of generalising. So, if I have picked on anyone, I've picked on the 'big boys' and I hope that they are big enough to forgive me. Great artists have their ups and downs. Only the mediocre are always at their best.

Fortunately I managed to secure the rights to reprint excerpts from the well-known worship song writer Kevin Molecule and I'd like to thank him and my good friend Dave Davey of Songs of Dwellingness Ministries, for permission to reprint some of their correspondence.

Kevin Molecule
27a Cinderpile Crescent
Stoke Poges

Mr Dave Davey
Songs of Dwellingness Ministries
Briglimpton
SUSSEX

Dear Mr Davey,

Wow! I am amazed and - I have to say - slightly
humbled by your response. Obviously I and the
people in the Stoke Poges Strict Tabernacle
have been aware of my gifting, but to have it
confirmed by you means a lot to me.

Yes, I do have some more worship songs.
Lots more in fact. And I find that I can pretty
much churn them out at the drop of a hat. I've
only got to open my Bible these days and the
song just leaps out at me!

You ask about worship in my church. Well,
we like to think that we are in the forefront
of the modern worship movement. Our songs and
approach are fresh and new; songs written by
the people for the people and in the people's
language. Like my song 'Balm of Gilead,
Blessings of Ramoth'.

There are always people in the church who
hark on about hymns and all that. My Dad is
a bit of a hymn freak and he keeps going on
at me about how great all hymns are and how
rubbish the electric guitar is. But I tell him
that we're in a new world now. Out with the
old! In with the new! I'm currently working on

one which is all about how amazing grace is.
I don't think that's been done before.

Anyway, here's one that the Lord gave to me
this morning on the way to work.

> **God is doing new things,**
> *All the time;*
> *Shiny new wineskins*
> *With shiny new wine.*
> *A new anointing,*
> *And new words to speak,*
> *I really hope my wineskin*
> *Will never spring a leak.*
>
> *Oh, heal our leaky wineskins,*
> *Restore our dried out lakes;*
> *We want to feel your Spirit,*
> *When the waters break.*

I played this to my Dad and I think he was really
moved. At any rate, he had to rush out of the
room suddenly. Mum said it was his age, but I
think he was responding to my anointingness.

With deep blessings,

Kevin Molecule
Worship Leader

How we got here: or
A brief history of worship music

Hymns – sacred poetry set to music – have always been a part of the Christian church. Quotations from early Christian hymns appear in Paul's letters[1] and Paul differentiates between hymns and psalms in Colossians 3:16 and Ephesians 5:19. So, the indication is that the early Christians sang their own lyrics and expressed the faith in their own words, as well as using the Scriptures set to music.

The earliest complete hymn we have was written by Clement of Alexandria in the second century and begins:

> Bridle of colts untamed,
> Over our wills presiding;
> Wing of unwandering birds,
> Our flight securely guiding.
> Rudder of youth unbending,
> Firm against adverse shock;
> Shepherd, with wisdom tending
> Lambs of the royal flock.

It's an interesting hymn, not least because of the wide range of imagery that Clement uses. As well as traditional images like lambs and shepherds, he uses a colt's bridle, bird's wings, a ship's rudder – all in the context of taming and guiding people.

---

[1] E.g. Eph. 5:14; 1 Tim. 3:16; 1 Tim. 6:15, 16; 2 Tim. 2:11–13.

Hymn-writing flourished in the third and fourth centuries and some of the hymns written then are still used today as part of the liturgy of the Orthodox Church. Hymns were used to praise God, to expound doctrine and even to refute heresies. They were part of the church's teaching, as much as anything else.

From the fifth century, however, authorities began to question whether any words other than Scripture should be allowed in worship. It was the start of an argument that was to last for more than a thousand years. Hymns were eventually admitted to the worship of the Roman Catholic Church in the thirteenth century, where they were used, not to express personal feelings, but to explain the meaning of what was going on.

Although the Reformation led to a burst of hymn-writing by Martin Luther and some of his followers, Calvinist churches refused to sing anything but the Scriptures; they would sing the Psalms, but nothing else. After the Reformation hit Britain, it was this Calvinist view which largely held sway. Psalms arranged for singing – what was known as the Metrical Psalter – were widely used, but other forms of singing were frowned upon.

(Opposition to hymns was not always based purely on theological grounds; George Wither's *Hymns and Songs of the Church* [1623] was suppressed by the Company of Stationers because the Company had the monopoly on printing the Metrical Psalter. The last thing they wanted was a best-selling hymn book disrupting their lucrative trade.)

So, by the early seventeenth century, hymn-writing had become a largely private occupation. Such hymns as were written were private expressions of faith, circulated mainly among the aristocracy and, if they were sung at all, they were sung in private chapels.

But in 1673 a Baptist minister called Benjamin Keach read the following in his Bible:

And when they had sung an hymn, they went out into the mount of Olives.

(Mt. 26:30, KJV)

'If it's good enough for Jesus', he thought, 'it should be good enough for us', and the next Sunday, he got his congregation to sing a hymn at the end of communion. Although this immediately caused a split in his denomination, Keach persisted and, in 1697, published *Spiritual Melody*, one of the first collections of Christian hymns intended for corporate worship.[2]

His example soon caught on. Forward-thinking pastors and church leaders saw that singing songs about God in their own language was a way of teaching people important truths. The arrival of the Methodists and the rise of the early evangelical church was a major factor in the success of congregational singing. The dominant theme in Methodism and evangelicalism was the personal experience of the saving power of Jesus – no wonder people wanted to sing songs and write poetry about it. Indeed, it was the eighteenth century that really saw the rise of hymns as we know them today.

The most famous of the early English hymn writers was Isaac Watts (1674–1748) who wrote over 400 hymns including famous ones like 'O God, Our Help in Ages Past' and 'When I Survey the Wondrous Cross'. Isaac

---

[2] Keach defended hymn-singing in his book *The Breach Repaired in God's Worship, or Singing of Psalms, Hymns and Spiritual Songs proved to be a Holy Ordinance of Jesus Christ* (London, 1697). What do you mean you haven't read it?

Watts wrote poetry to 'express the spiritual experience of the singer'.[3]

Watts saw hymns as more than just the repetition of Scripture. He believed that authentic Christian worship had to include original, personal expressions of faith. It was Watts, more than any other man, who established the model for the hymns that we sing today.

Crucially, he saw his task as writing for ordinary people. He wrote:

> I would neither indulge any bold metaphors, nor admit of hard words, nor tempt the ignorant worshipper to sing without his understanding.[4]

He admitted that this was a difficult task to 'sink every line to the level of a whole congregation' while still turning out something that was technically and critically good.

This theme was taken up by John Newton, the author of hymns such as 'Amazing Grace' and 'How Sweet the Name of Jesus Sounds', who wrote:

> There is a style and manner suited to the composition of hymns which may be more successfully or at least more easily attained by a versifier than a poet. They should be Hymns not Odes, if designed for public worship, and for the use of plain people. Perspicuity, simplicity, and ease, should chiefly be attended to; and the imagery and colouring of poetry, if admitted at all, should be indulged in very sparingly, and with great judgment.[5]

---

[3] F. Cross (ed.), *Oxford Dictionary of the Christian Church* (Oxford: OUP, 1983), p. 683.

[4] Quoted in Andrew Wilson-Dickson, *A Brief History of Christian Music, from Biblical Times to the Present* (Oxford: Lion Publishing, 1997), p. 179.

[5] John Newton and William Cowper, *Olney Hymns* (London, 1788), p. iii.

Meanwhile, in the Methodist church, Charles Wesley, working with his brother John, wrote around 6,500 hymns. The Methodists insisted that their music should be accessible and simple. John Wesley's *Collection of Psalms and Hymns* appeared in 1723, followed by *Hymns and Sacred Psalms*, by John and his brother Charles in 1739.

John Wesley was even happy to adapt popular tunes of the day to use Christian lyrics – much to the disapproval of his opponents. He even provided seven rules for congregational singing, which included 'singing lustily and with good courage', not singing too loudly and drowning out other people, singing in time and

> Above all, sing spiritually. Have an eye to God in every word you sing. Aim at pleasing him more than yourself.[6]

Not a bad rule that.

Hymn-singing soon spread through the non-conformist churches and through the evangelical wing of the Anglican Church, despite the fact that the church authorities disapproved of the practice.[7]

In America, one of the earliest expressions of hymn-writing was the spiritual, which grew out of the suffering and slavery of black African-Americans. These songs reflected the reality of their situation.

> Oh, my Lord!
> Oh, my good Lord!
> Keep me from sinkin' down.
> I tell you what I mean to do
> (Keep me from sinkin' down)

---

[6] Wesley, *Select Hymns* (London, 1761).
[7] Even as late as 1890, the use of hymns was still a cause of dispute in the Anglican Church.

> I mean to go to heaven too
> (Keep me from sinkin' down)
> I look up yonder and what do I see?
> (Keep me from sinkin' down)
> I see the angels beckonin' me
> (Keep me from sinkin' down).[8]

Although they drew heavily on Scripture, the language was that of the ordinary, suffering slave:

> They crucified my Lord an' he
> never said a mumbalin' word.

The songs even contained coded references to underground escape networks and even criticised the hypocrisy of the white Christian slave owners:

> Everybody talkin' about
> Heaven ain't goin' there …

Through these hymns, the slaves often identified themselves with the Israelites in Egypt; the chosen people, enslaved and awaiting freedom. Their songs comforted them and reassured them that God had not forgotten them. Their masters might have told them that they were sub-human; but they knew that one day, God would set them free.

Gradually, even the monolithic monster that was the Anglican Church absorbed hymn-singing into its regular pattern of worship. The Anglicans put together their 'official' hymn book – *Hymns Ancient and Modern* – in 1861, and by the turn of the century 60 million copies had been sold.

---

[8] Words assumed to be in the public domain – the authors of spirituals would have been anonymous and the publication originally in the nineteenth century.

New movements of God created new music. On both sides of the Atlantic, revival was accompanied by new bursts of hymn-writing. Hymns such as those of Moody and Sankey – hymns which were designed for mission and evangelism – were hugely popular and influential, on both sides of the Atlantic.

And, as more new movements arose, more hymns flooded onto the market, and more new music as well. The fact is that, throughout history, every renewal movement within the church – whatever the denomination – has been accompanied by new songs. Especially, with songs that are accessible to the common man and woman. William Booth, founder of this Salvation Army, grasped the need to use popular music and images. Sally Army tunes had something of the music hall about them; they appealed to the common person. Like Wesley before him, Booth even adapted lyrics to fit with the popular secular songs of his day.

By the end of the nineteenth century, hymn-writing had become a major industry. Hymns were churned out at an astonishing rate. Henry Gauntlett, who wrote the words to 'Once in Royal David's City', wrote around 10,000 other hymns.[9] Percy Dearmer calculated that there were some 400,000 hymns in use at the end of the nineteenth century. Of these, only sixteen were in all hymn books and fifty in each of the six most popular hymn books. Dearmer reckoned that out of the 400,000 there were only about 200 really fine hymns.[10]

The result of this hymn overload was a kind of musical fight to the death, a survival of the fittest, what J.R. Watson calls 'hymnological Darwinism'.[11] Hymns which were little

[9] Andrew Wilson-Dickson, *A Brief History of Christian Music*, p. 229.
[10] Percy Dearmer, *Songs of Praise* (London: OUP, 1925), pp. iii–iv.
[11] J.R. Watson, *The English Hymn* (Oxford: OUP, 1997), pp. 340–6.

sung have been forgotten, left out of modern collections.
Gradually they were discarded. The hymns we still sing
today are the cream of the crop, the very best examples of a
tradition which grew from ordinary people using ordinary
words to express their extraordinary faith.

Revival and renewal

By the mid-twentieth century, however, hymns had begun
to ossify. The new movements which had fuelled the music
of the church had dried up. There was little in the way
of new song writing and disquiet about the standard,
denominational collections of hymns was beginning to
grow.

In the 1950s, an organisation called The Twentieth
Century Light Music Group argued that

> not only the great and lasting music of the past but also
> the ordinary and transient music of today – which is the
> background to the lives of so many – has a rightful place in
> our worship.[12]

The music they were talking about was foxtrots and
waltzes and popular dance and their words were taken
up by the adherents of other forms of popular music. The
1960s folk song revival, for example, was the background
for books like *Youth Praise*. In the era of Elvis and the Beatles
and the Stones, singing hymns to the organ was not, like,
where it's at, man.

So when the charismatic renewal swept through the
churches in the 1970s, the ground had been laid for a
remarkable upsurge of musical creativity and for the

---

[12] Quoted in Wilson-Dickson, *A Brief History of Christian Music*, p.
412.

canonisation of the guitar. There were musicals like *If My People* and *Dunamis* by Jimmy and Carol Owens. There were choruses all over the place.

Like the hymns sung by Benjamin Keach and his congregation some 300 years earlier, these were songs from and for the people. They were vernacular expressions of faith. While hymn-writing had gradually ossified into an 'authorised' practice, with hymns collected and issued by committees of the great and the good, the charismatic renewal blew all those distinctions out of the water. Here, churches began to sing what they liked, from wherever they found it.

It was a wonderful democratisation of worship. No longer was worship the province of trained organists and choir-directors, it was now open to anyone who could strum a guitar or bash a drumset. (This, too, was more of a link with the past than they recognised, since, in the days before the organ became the Blest Instrument Of Worship, many churches had their own, home-grown orchestras.)

Gradually these new songs were drawn together in collections – perhaps the most famous being *Songs of Fellowship* and *Mission Praise*, both of which are still in widespread use today. Songs produced by Soul Survivor, by the Vineyard churches, by the Australian Hillsongs movement, the one-man industry that is known as Graham Kendrick, the New Frontiers churches, the Iona Community, Spring Harvest – all these produce many hundreds of worship songs each year.

Worship song writing, like hymn-writing before it, has become an industry. Books such as *Songs of Fellowship*, the numerous Spring Harvest song books and the Soul Survivor song books sell by their thousands. Events and conferences with their 'times of worship' have created a demand for – and a showcase for – new songs. Worship leaders bring out their work on CDs. Hymn books sold by the millions; new worship collections do the same.

The worship song is the hymn's younger brother. Like the hymn, it has been born from renewal; like the hymn it has become an industry; like the hymn it is intended as a vernacular expression of a personal faith. Worship songs live and work in this tradition.

Hymns were always intended to be multi-purpose. They were never intended just to be pure repetitions of Scripture. They were meant to inspire, encourage, challenge and teach Christians. They addressed contemporary issues and problems. They allowed Christians to identify with characters and situations in the Bible. They were emotional responses to the truth of God. They were part of the reality of the world around them.

The real question is how well are worship songs dealing with this part of their inheritance? Certainly in terms of volume, the worship song can be said to be hugely successful. But are modern worship songs teaching the church? Are they engaging with reality? Are they actually speaking the language of the people?

Or are they increasingly ephemeral, fleeting creations which do little more than repeat Scripture or stir a brief emotion? Whatever the faults of the hymns, many hymns have survived – some for more than 300 years. Looking at today's worship songs, however, one has to wonder how many will be around in three years, let alone 300.

It may be that those who write worship songs are unaware even that they should be doing things like using worship songs to teach the church or engage with reality. Or it may be that they're unable to do it. Or it may be something more serious; it may be that we need to go right back to basics and look at what worship actually is.

Key points

- Hymns and worship songs have always been a part of the Christian church.

- From the beginning, Christians used the hymn form to express their faith in their own words and images.

- Great hymn writers saw hymns as original, personal expressions of Christian faith.

- Hymns were intended to be accessible and simple.

- The best hymns have always used the language of the people.

Key questions

- How many of today's worship songs will still be sung in 200 years' time?

- Are we sacrificing quality of worship songs for quantity of output?

- How well do worship songs teach the church?

- How far do they speak in the language of the people?

Kevin Molecule
27a Cinderpile Crescent
Stoke Poges

Mr Dave Davey
Songs of Dwellingness Ministries
Briglimpton
SUSSEX

Dear Brother Davey,

Thanks for your comments on the latest CD.
I'm really glad that the music 'put you in
the mood for worship, even though you were
stuck on the A2 going home'.

That's a key part of what we want to do
as a worship band; we want the music to
speak. The people in the Tabernacle really
get into the emotion of worshipping when
we play. I suppose it's an anointing thing,
really.

Anyway, I've tried to reflect that in some
of my worship songs. You know, keep them
simple and not let the words get in the way
of the worship. Let the music do the job. I
don't think people need to think in worship;
they need to feel. I don't think that
thoughts are what we want people to think;
but feelings are what we want people to feel.
What do you think?

Anyway, in the light of that, here is
my latest outpouring. It's a simple chant
that will just let the emotions do their
work.

Isn't he holy? I reckon he is.
His holiness fills every minute.
He's holy and holy; oh holy is he,
God is pure holiness, innit?

Chorus
He's so holy,
Holy, holy, holy,
Holy, holy, holy, etc.
(Repeat until blessed)

With deep reflection,

Kevin Molecule
Worship Leader

But they're only words: or
Why worship matters

As the nineteenth-century hymn explosion shows, quantity is not necessarily quality. Musically, everything in the garden is rosy. Musically, the church is benefiting from the experience and expertise of a great many talented musicians and composers.

Lyrically, however, things are different. Lyrically, I think we've drifted away. We've lost the plot in a number of ways. It's not just the strange language and the problems with technique, although these are serious issues which I shall be dealing with later. Fundamentally, faults of language and technique spring from a much more deep-rooted problem. Fundamentally, the problems with so much modern worship song writing stem, I believe, from a serious misconception of what worship actually is.

Worship is much, much more than singing a few songs. It's much more than getting in a good mood. It's much more than chanting a few verses from the Bible.

It's real life.

Worship is real life

It's popular in many churches to talk of 'times of worship'. 'Now we'll have a time of worship,' says the leader at the front, before introducing a series of songs which can last for anything from 15 minutes to 15 hours. Strange that. Because you might as well talk about having a 'time of breathing' or a 'time of just being ourselves'. Worship – true worship – is not about singing songs, or holding up your hands or bouncing up and down or chanting Gregorian plainsong. It's about how you live your life.

In John 4, Jesus is in Samaria. When he encounters a Samaritan woman at a well, she tries to engage him in a discussion about the relative values of different kinds of worship. In a vain attempt to get away from his challenging, personal questions, she asks him whether true worship takes place on Mount Gerizim – the sacred place of the Samaritans – or in the temple in Jerusalem.

Jesus replies,

> Believe me, the time is coming when you won't worship the Father either on this mountain or in Jerusalem. You Samaritans don't really know the one you worship. But we Jews do know the God we worship, and by using us, God will save the world. But a time is coming, and it is already here! Even now the true worshippers are being led by the Spirit to worship the Father according to the truth. These are the ones the Father is seeking to worship him.
>
> (Jn. 4:21–23, CEV)

This is a significant answer, even though the question was probably not asked with the same sense of importance. Worship, Jesus says, is not a matter of place. It's not where you worship, or when you worship, it's a question of knowing God and living in truth. If you know the truth and respond to that, then you are worshipping. That's what worship is: a response to the truth.[1]

We worship by the way we live. We are led by the Spirit to acknowledge Jesus as our Lord and follow his commands.

---

[1] For a more detailed exploration of this passage, see Vaughan Roberts, *True Worship* (Carlisle: Authentic Lifestyle, 2002), pp. 1–13.

So you cannot separate off worship from the rest of the Christian life. The idea that 'worship' is something that only takes place in a church or at a conference – and then only in a 'time of worship' is profoundly unbiblical. Worship – showing God how much we value him, how much he is worth to us – is an attitude of life. Worship, putting it simply, means showing Jesus what we think of him. And we do that not only by singing songs about him, but by changing our lives so that they reflect our new master.

Worship is life. It's not a bloke up the front with the guitar; it's not a choir singing an oratorio; it's not men in fancy dress swinging incense around. Those are expressions of worship, it is true, but worship is much, much bigger than that.

Now this may seem to be a very basic theological point; but the point is that this identification of 'singing' with 'worship' means that the whole process has become isolated from the rest of our life. Worship has become an event, an occasion, isolated and distinct from the rest of our life and from our real walk with God. And when we 'split off' worship in this way, then it becomes easier to accept that the worship times will be markedly different from the rest of our life. They will have a different language, a different feel. You can use language that you would never dream of using in your real life because this isn't real life; it's a *time of worship.* By identifying church services as 'Sunday worship' and the church itself as 'a place of worship' we can segregate them from our real life.

The result is a kind of bubble in our Christian lives. There is our real life – our time at work or with our family or at college or at school; and there is our worship life, lived in church, involving a lot of singing, and mainly expressed in the kind of language we would never use anywhere else.

And people go to church and wonder what connection all this has with the rest of their life.

As Willard Sperry said,

> Every man [*sic*] who habitually goes to church finds himself again and again provided with vehicles for his worship which he has the greatest reluctance to use, either because he doubts their truth or because they have no correspondence with his own experience.[2]

Sperry was writing in the 1920s, but the problem is still acute today. Don't believe me? Well, think for a moment about the kinds of things you say and sing during worship.

If, sitting in your own home, I asked you to tell me about God, what would you say? Perhaps you'd tell me that God loves me. Perhaps you'd tell me how he came to earth as Jesus and how Jesus died for us. Maybe you'd tell me about your relationship with God; how he guides you and supports you.

All well and good. I doubt, however, that you'd tell me that 'his glory fills the temple'. I very much doubt you'd tell me that he 'redeemed' you, or that he lifted you from the 'mirey clay'. You wouldn't use that kind of language. Because that's 'worship' language.

This distinction both in our attitude towards worship and in the language we use during worship can lead us into singing things that we wouldn't dream of saying.

Someone once wrote, 'When I became a Christian I stopped telling lies and started singing them.' We make much more outrageous statements in song than we would in speech. Who among us has not vowed to make history?

[2] Willard Sperry, *Reality in Worship: A study of public worship and private religion* (New York: Macmillan, 1925), p. 203.

Who has promised to build with silver and gold?[3] Or stated that our problems all disappear in Jesus' presence? Or that we want to give everything we have to the Lord? These are all laudable statements, but I can't help thinking if we were asked to say them, rather than sing them, we might think a little more carefully about what we were actually promising.[4] When I was young there used to be a popular children's hymn in the singing of which we all committed ourselves to being eaten by large wild animals. If you ask someone, 'Would you mind being eaten alive by a large hairy animal as part of your faith?' I wonder what they'd reply.

We'll explore this aspect of worship song language more in a later chapter. For the moment, we have to recognise that worship is not something we do at certain points during the week; it's something that we live from day to day. So worship has to be real. It has to reflect and draw on the reality that surrounds us. It has to be connected to real life, because worship is real life.

As Willard Sperry put it,

> Worship is a deliberate and disciplined adventure in reality.[5]

This misunderstanding of the nature of worship – of the fact that it is our whole life – leads us to place far too much emphasis on the singing of worship songs. Because we

---

[3] This means, I think, to pay for the building. Not to build with big silver and gold bricks.

[4] Actually the willingness of people to sing anything in songs could be a source of useful revenue. I may just write a song with the line in it: 'I really want to serve God's plans in every single way / And give Nick Page 20 per cent of my net earnings on my next pay day.'

[5] Willard Sperry, quoted in Richard Foster, *Celebration of Discipline* (London: Hodder & Stoughton, 1980), p. 149.

identify that activity with worship. That is worship. So you have worship conferences, worship sessions, times of worship – but this is to mistake form for substance. Singing is not worship; it is only the place where worship can occur.

Real worship stems from a conscious decision to live our lives in God's way. It's not about singing; it's about living.

Worship is a response to God

The singing of worship songs is not worship. Worship is the recognition of what God is worth and the response to that fact.

Here's what Paul says in Romans:

> Dear friends, God is good. So I beg you to offer your bodies to him as a living sacrifice, pure and pleasing. That's the most sensible way to serve God.

(Rom. 12:1, CEV)

What Paul is saying is that offering a sacrifice to God – an act of worship – is the logical response to who he is. God is good, he begins, and because of that everything else follows. The word translated as 'sensible' above is *logikos*, from which we get the word logic. Our worship, therefore, is a conscious response to what God has done for us.

True worship is a response to God. It arises from remembering what God has done for us, when we recognise that God took human form and died for us. This is not an act of emotion – although no doubt our response to this sacrifice should be emotional; it's a memory, an understanding. It's a matter of comprehension.

This is a theme that runs right to the very heart of the Bible. When God makes a covenant with his people he calls on them to follow him because of what he has already done. In the introduction to the Ten Commandments, God says,

> I am the LORD your God, the one who brought you out of Egypt where you were slaves.
>
> (Ex. 20:2, CEV)

God has already done the rescuing bit. Now he's looking for a response. The Israelites should obey him, not because of what he's going to do for them, but out of gratitude for what he has already done. The same is true of the Christian life. We should obey God, we should worship God, as a response to his love.

This is one of the key reasons why the words of our worship songs are so important: they should remind us why we worship God. If worship is a response to God's love we need to remember what God's love has done for us. And that needs to be expressed in words.

Worship, in this sense, is a deliberate, conscious act. It is an intellectual act. I don't mean by that, of course, that it's something for academics and 'deep thinkers'; I don't mean that it should be complicated or full of jargon or complex theological argument or anything like that. I mean that worship involves your brain. It involves the intellect; thinking about God and what he has done for you. That can be done in the simplest of language; indeed probably *should* be done in the simplest of language. One of the great difficulties of writing worship songs is to keep the language simple but the implications immense. The songs should have a weight to them, a substance that does not rely on long words or complicated theorems but on a deep and profound expression of the truth about God.

Worship is a response to the truth about God. As Richard Foster puts it: 'Worship is human response to divine initiative.'[6] Worship springs from thinking about God, from contemplation and meditation on who God is. This intellectual content, this need for the mind to focus on truth, is one of the things that distinguishes Christian worship from worship in many Eastern religions.

In a lot of Eastern religion, the aim is to empty the mind; to encounter the divine on a level that is almost subconscious. Mantras, yoga positions, even Zen koans are used to clear the mind of conscious thoughts and to encounter the divine.

But that's not what Christian worship is about. Christian worship is not about emptying the mind, but about filling the mind with God. Eastern meditation aims to detach us from the miserable state of existence. Christian worship reminds us that God thought so much of this material world he became a part of it. Eastern mysticism is all about becoming detached from the world; Christian worship is all about becoming attached to God.

The sad thing is that this Eastern philosophy has affected our worship. Sometimes singing songs over and over again becomes like chanting a mantra. I recall being in a 'worship session' in the late 1980s when we sang a song over and over and over and over again. It had three verses, this song. We sang each verse four times. Then we sang the whole thing again. Twice. Looking back, the mind entered a certain numbness. Consciousness certainly started to drift away at that point, although so did the will to live.

What this worship leader did was to confuse activity with worship. Just because a song is sung over and over again doesn't mean that the singers are worshipping. Without something of substance in the song, without something for

---

[6] Richard Foster, *Celebration of Discipline*, p. 138.

the mind to bite on, there can be no true worship. Without truth to feed on, worship will starve to death.

This is why the words of worship songs matter. They convey the truth – the truth to which we are supposed to respond. They aren't just sounds to enable us to join in the melody. They are the means by which the mind understands what God has done for us.

It follows that the more truth that the songs contain, the better expressed that truth is, the greater the response. Deep truths create deep worship. Shallow words create shallow worship. Banal, meaningless lyrics, badly crafted and expressed in confusing language, will not lead us into the deep worship that our world and our church need to see.

Richard Foster opened his influential book *Celebration of Discipline* with the words,

> Superficiality is the curse of our age. The doctrine of instant satisfaction is a primary spiritual problem. The desperate need today is not for a greater number of intelligent people, or gifted people, but for deep people.[7]

I think the same is true of worship. To paraphrase Foster, what we need today are not clever worship songs, nor informal worship songs, but *deep* worship songs. We need worship songs to really bring home the truth about God to us; worship songs that have sprung from deep meditation. We need pathways into God laid down by people who have already walked the path. A worship song should have depth. It is not a superficial high, intended for instant consumption and then disposed of. It is – or should be – an offering to God. Not something that was knocked off in half an hour on the back of a notice sheet.

---

[7] Richard Foster, *Celebration of Discipline*, p. 1.

But the fact is that so many of the songs we sing today are instantly forgettable and instantly disposable. They are disposable because they are not the product of deep contemplation and they are not the product of skill and craft. Too often the words to our worship songs feel like a kind of added extra to the music. If they have a telling phrase or a striking image that's a rare bonus. Most of the time they seem to be there just so everyone has a chance to join in.

It is not taking part in the activity, or attending the conference that makes us worshippers; it is a recognition of what God has done for us and a determination to repay his love by living in his way. Worship is responding to the truth. And in order to worship deeply we have to feed on deep truth.

Worship is feeling and thinking

Worship is more than just words, however. It's not just a dry, academic recognition of fact. It's also about *feeling* the truth.

This, I think, is where the real strength of worship songs come in. Because music enables us to add emotion to understanding; it helps us to feel the truth. A triumphant song will make us feel more triumphant. A sad song will make us feel more sad. Music enhances the emotive power of the words.

Worship songs aim to help the singer to experience the close presence of God. It is not that God is not present with them at other times; it is that through singing songs we experience him both emotionally and intellectually. We understand more about him; and we feel more about him.

The problem is that, if the words aren't giving us any deep truth, then the emotion is all we've got. And, while emotion is important, feelings fade. The music eventually comes to an end.

What worship songs and hymns can do in a manner that is unlike any other is to express those truths in immediate, identifiable ways. Worship songs can bring together words and music to help people identify, take hold of and respond to truth. John Middleton Murry paints a picture of someone reading a poem:

> We have had emotions like them before, but never so power-
> fully, never with such a sense of their unity; before they were
> dishevelled, now they are coherent, before they were vague,
> now they are clear.[8]

Worship songs at their best are like this. Oh, yes, we know theoretically that God loves us, but when we sing that song, we both know *and* feel it. Before we might have dimly perceived what Jesus' sacrifice was like, but the words of that song and the emotion of the tune make it so much clearer. They bring home the truth, they drive it deep into our hearts and we respond with worship.

As I hope to show, there are few areas of church life which have more potential to make us think and feel than sung worship. It brings together the emotional and the intellectual; it makes us think and feel. And when we understand the truth both intellectually and emotionally, when we feel in our bones what we know to be true, then that has to result in worship.

---

[8] Quoted in Sperry, *Reality in Worship*, p. 237.

Key points

- Our worship of God is expressed through how we live. It is real life. So worship songs should relate to our real-life walk with God.

- Our worship of God is a response to the truth about him. So worship songs should seek to embody the truth in ways we can understand. And the deeper the truth, the deeper the worship.

- Our worship of God is both intellectual and emotional. Worship songs play a unique part in helping us to feel what we know to be true.

Key questions

- Does our worship relate to our real life? Do the songs we write relate to the real experiences and lives of Christians?

- Do our worship songs spring from contemplation? Do they spring from our own experience? Does our Bible study, our prayer life, our everyday experience inform our song writing?

- Do we confuse singing with worship?

Kevin Molecule
27a Cinderpile Crescent
Stoke Poges

Mr Dave Davey
Songs of Dwellingness Ministries
Briglimpton
SUSSEX

Dear Dave,

Please find enclosed the pictures you were asking about. The first one could go on the cover, I suppose. It shows me walking down a street carrying my guitar above my head and has that kind of grainy, moody look that we were after.

The second shows me and the band in action at the 'Wild Worship' festival last summer. As you can see the light show and special effects were pretty impressive! We had fireworks that showed up in the shape of a cross. (Well, they would have showed properly if the bolts hadn't come loose. But you'll be pleased to know that Josh the drummer has recovered now and the nurse says that in a few years the burns won't hardly show at all.)

You asked whether the rest of my band write songs, to which the answer is 'no'. They don't have my anointing. Some of them have expressed an interest in writing some words, but I feel I have to keep this 'in house' as it were. I believe my words and music are intimately tied together. If I were to get someone else involved in that it would get more complicated.

Anyway, I think that my audience expect to sing Kevin Molecule songs. That's what they come for after all. Anything else would be a disappointment.

Talking of which, here's my latest. I've gone for a deliberately funky, up-to-the-minute feel on this. In fact, when I perform this song live, I also bung in a rap section.

> ***Ooh you are so good,***
> *I'm gonna clap my hands,*
> *I just wanna praise you*
> *And conquer heathen lands.*
> *You're so amazing*
> *Your love will never die*
> *Come on everybody!*
> *Lai-lai-lai-lai-lai!*
>
> **Chorus**
> *Lai-lai-lai-lai-lai, etc.*

With deep joy,

Kevin Molecule
Worship Leader

From poet to pop star: or
How we got into this mess

We have seen that worship is a fundamental part of life and that it's a response to God's truth. We have seen, therefore, the key role that worship songs have in communicating that truth.

So how did we get here? How did we get to a point where the fundamental seriousness of worship was being undermined by the overwhelming banality of the words?

Whatever happened to worship?

From poem to pop song

Part of the problem is that we have changed from the poetry approach to the pop singer model.

In previous times, hymns didn't just inspire worship, they taught the congregations something about God. Indeed, the first hymns were not written to be sung; they were poems intended to be read and thought about. A hymn writer like John Newton would use his lyrics to form the themes of his sermons. People bought books of hymns to read, as well as sing.

Hymns were the products of a society where poetry was still a major art form. Poets such as Wordsworth and Tennyson and Byron were major public figures and their books were purchased by the cartload. Hymn writers published their work as books of poetry to be read and pondered on. Sometimes, admittedly, the hymns weren't worth the pondering, but that's not the point. The point is that the hymn writers were wordsmiths. Isaac Watts and Charles Wesley did not write the music; they were lyricists. They were poets in a time when poetry was a major art form.

Nowadays poetry is, if not dead, then in the intensive care unit. We still have a poet laureate but books of poetry are rarely published and generally meet only a minority audience. (Of course there are times when poetry reaches out beyond that. The reading of a poem during the funeral scene in *Four Weddings and a Funeral* propelled Auden's verse back into the best-seller lists many years after his death. The Poetry on the Underground project has been a huge success. But poetry is very much a minority sport these days.)

Today the predominant model for verse-writing is the pop song. Poetry might be struggling, but rock and roll is here to stay. Today's worship songs are written by people steeped in pop and rock music traditions. Songs are not published as poems to be read, but tunes to be played. The spiral binding has replaced the leather-bound book. So the model for the hymn was the poem; but the model for the worship song is the pop song.

This is a huge change. Pop brings with it its own views of the lyric. In poetry, what matters is the words – the metaphors, the images, the rhythm and the structure. In pop songs what matters is the melody, the hook, the beat. Having a decent lyric is a bonus. Pop songs want a tune that sticks in your brain. It doesn't matter to them if the lyrics are nothing more than 'A wop-bop-a-lu-bam-bop'. What matters is that the tune is catchy and the rhythm makes you dance.

Pop songs are nuggets of emotion. A pop song, generally speaking, is not about deep thought, but intense feeling. It's not supposed to challenge you or inspire you or lead you into deep truth; it's supposed to make you feel happy or sad. Or both at once. Pop songs place more emphasis on the melody and the beat than on the words, most of which use the same vocabulary and cover the same themes.

Of course there are exceptions to the rule. I belong to a generation that saw the pop format break out of the disposable, throw-away song and into the realm of real art and I will beat to a pulp anyone who says that the Beatles were not great artists. Generally speaking, however, the pop song is a disposable item intended to give you an emotional rush. The pop world is a world of banal emotion and meaningless lyrics – and I speak as a man who still buys a lot of pop and rock music. After all, how many truly memorable pop lyrics can you remember from the last ten years? We live in a superficial, shallow culture and our media reflects that. In an era of banality, the banal lyric is hardly noticeable. We don't expect a song to challenge us or inspire us any more. We just want to feel good.

The same is true of too many modern worship songs. The words often seem second in importance to the music. They talk about the same things in the same way. And often, we end up singing little more than the religious equivalent of 'I love you baby, oh yeah'.

They're pop songs, where the lyric is secondary to the melody; where the emphasis is on provoking an emotional response rather than an intellectual one. The move from the poetry model to the pop model is a move from thoughtful reflection to disposable emotion. We don't publish the words of our worship songs as poetry collections today, not only because people don't read poems, but because these poems are not worth reading.

I would guess that most lyrics are written after the melody has been written. And I would also guess that the melody is the key to the song's survival. If it's got a decent tune, it'll be more likely to survive. How often, I wonder, have good words been discarded because the tune didn't turn out to be popular? This is different to the history of hymns, where a good hymn lyric might be around for years before finding an appropriate tune. For example, 'Amazing Grace' had many different tunes applied to it, and only settled on the tune we know and love some fifty years after the lyric was written. What mattered was that people recognised the quality of the words and were determined to see them used.

It's not just that worship song lyrics don't last; the suspicion is that no one expects them to last. They're not crafted with any expectation or hope of longevity; they're written on the understanding that they will suffer a quick death. They're the spiritual equivalent of the paper plate. They serve their purpose, but it's time to throw away the old and move on. This is a consumerist, superficial view of worship; the idea that once a song has been used up we can throw it away. The idea of dwelling on a lyric, of contemplating it, is almost unimaginable. What is there to contemplate? It's a disposable product.

We have a church that is addicted to newness, part of a culture which worships continuous consumption, and in the pop song we have found the perfect model for the easy-come, easy-go worship song. What's top of the charts this week will be forgotten next week; don't worry if you've forgotten the words of the song you've just sung, there'll be another one along in a minute. It's fast-food worship; fine at the time, but half an hour later you feel hungry all over again.

The rise of the singer-songwriter

So, we're living in a pop-song world. The model for the worship song is not the poem with its emphasis on thought, but the pop song with its emphasis on emotion.

However, this doesn't explain why so many songs are so badly written. After all, many popular songs are superbly crafted and lyrically sophisticated. They have phrases that stick in the memory. They have rhyme schemes that work. Indeed, many performers are rediscovering the great songs. A new generation of jazz singers are breaking out the old standards, and finding them to be refreshingly well made. From Robbie Williams in the Albert Hall to Katie Melua in Ronnie Scott's, there is a resurgence of interest in the traditional, crafted song.

The problem is that, along with adopting the model of the pop song, we've also adopted the model of the singer-songwriter.

We have already seen how the great hymn writers were lyricists not composers. Up until fairly recently the same was true for most popular music. It was common for songs to be the product of teams – usually a composer and a lyricist. There were teams like Rodgers and Hart, George and Ira Gershwin; there were lyricists like Sammy Cahn and Don Black. These people were trained in lyric writing; they spent their lives searching for the perfect rhyme, the telling phrase. Musicals, where the songs have to convey a lot of information, are still generally produced this way.

But in the pop world, things changed. Elvis had his songs written for him; but the Beatles and Bob Dylan did the job themselves. And ever since then, if you're a serious musician, a serious pop star, you write your own stuff. The trouble is that very few singer-songwriters are genuinely good lyric writers. Very few people are Bob Dylan or the Beatles. Most singer-songwriters are better musicians than poets, they're better at the tunes than at the words. But that never stops them. In a world where words don't matter so much, composers are much more likely to write their own lyrics. After all, if no one cares what they're singing, then it doesn't matter what I write. And anyway, these are my songs; my lyrics. So there.

Anyway, there are problems with a lyricist. You have to share the writing credit (and the royalties). You have to work as a partnership. It's the tune that really matters ... And anyway, how hard can it be?

Worship song writing has bought into this model big time. In one recent collection of songs, nearly 90 per cent were written by individuals. Specialist lyricists are rare. The singer-songwriter reigns supreme.

But lyric writing is not a subsidiary art. It's not something that 'anyone can do'. As Andy Piercy says,

> I am beginning to think that writing worship songs is far too important to leave to just the singers and musicians. For some reason, contemporary worship music seems to have unquestioningly taken on board the rock and pop model of the singer/songwriter, and so assumes that the singer/ musician should be the one to write both the words and music of the song. Why?[1]

Why indeed? Where are the lyricists in our church? Where are the wordsmiths, the poets, the 'versifiers' to use Newton's term? They must be there. And it's up to those who write the tunes to give them a chance.

From hymn to 'me'

So the lyric has been downgraded. It's no longer such an important part of the worship. As long as the music makes you feel the right way, the lyric can be anything. We can

---

[1] Matt Redman (ed.), *Heart of Worship Files* (Eastbourne: Kingsway Communications, 2003), p. 98.

fool ourselves into thinking that we're worshipping God
when all we're doing is getting an emotional rush from
the guitar solo.

As D.M. Lloyd Jones said,

> … you can become drunk on singing: you can go on singing
> and singing until, really, you are in such an emotional state
> that your mind is no longer operating.[2]

I'm not knocking emotion. As we saw in the last chapter,
emotion is part of our response to God. A non-emotional
Christian is someone who has forgotten how to feel; but,
equally, a completely emotional Christian is someone who
has forgotten how to think.

Too often times of worship are judged, not on whether
people were changed or challenged or renewed, but on
the response of the crowd, the 'buzz' in the building.
This is not a reliable indicator of the presence of God.
I frequently feel intense emotions when Watford score
a goal.[3] But I wouldn't claim that God had much to do
with it.

Emotion, by its very nature, is personal, intimate.
Perhaps that is one of the reasons why so much of worship
– indeed religion in general – has been turning in on itself.
If what I feel is all that matters, then that will be reflected
in the words that I sing and the style of my worship. The
result is that we have worship songs that concentrate
almost solely on us as individuals and, more specifically,
on how we feel. Our worship songs are more about creating
feeling rather than helping understanding. Songs talk less

---

[2] D.M. Lloyd-Jones, *Singing to the Lord* (Bridgend, Wales: Bryntirion
Press, 2003), p. 37.

[3] All right, not frequently. But we do occasionally put the ball in the
net.

and less about the attributes of God, or the work of Jesus, and more about, well, *me*.

You cannot read a modern collection of worship songs without noticing the prominent use of 'I' or 'me'. In one collection I estimated that over half the songs were to do with the individual and the individual's relationship with God.

Obviously this is not wrong in itself; the same mode of expression can be found in many psalms. But when so many songs talk about 'I', when phrases such as 'I want', or 'make me' or 'give me' arrive in such numbers, it is difficult to escape the feeling that I should only be interested in God for how he makes me feel.

Hymns and worship songs are corporate affairs. They are designed to be sung by more than one person; by a body of people, in fact. And they are designed to point those people towards God. At the beginning of this book I wrote how hymns were intended to instruct and teach. Maybe they went far too much towards that end of the scale. Certainly remembering my upbringing I can't remember getting very excited over the contents of the *Baptist Hymnal*, but equally I can remember many times more recently when, during worship, I have been urged to become very excited over, well, nothing in particular. If worship of forty years ago had ossified into unemotional intellectualising, then it is equally true that much of today's worship has leapt headlong into mindless emotionalism.

We need balance. As I argued earlier, worship is a combination of understanding and feeling: when we understand what God has done for us and who he is, then the emotion should follow. Understanding alone results in lifeless, dry worship. Emotion alone results in superficial, temporary worship. We need a balanced diet.

Worship songs are objective truth as well as subjective expression. They should contain truth about God, not just statements about how we feel. Worship songs should surely fix on the object of worship, rather than the one worshipping, but at times it's hard to see even a speck of God for the great beam of self-obsession obscuring the view.

Many worship song leaders are, I believe, responding to this and moving back to the real focus. Perhaps the most eloquent expression of this is Matt Redman's song 'When the music fades' with its identification that the focus of our worship is, or should be, Jesus.[4] He's absolutely right. In a world where so much worship is about me, we would do well to remember that it's really all about him.

From corporate singing to pop concert

The pop-music aesthetic is all about entertainment. It's about a three-minute single that makes you feel great; it's about a pulsing beat that fills the dance floor; it's about a stage show with lights and laser beams. It's about *performance.*

Leading sung worship is not like playing a pop concert. Or it shouldn't be. It's not about feeling the buzz of the crowd; it's about feeling the presence of God. I'm certainly not against good musicianship or attempting to create the right atmosphere. But good musicianship is not a replacement for worship; and a great performance is no certain indicator of the presence of God.

Worship at events like Spring Harvest and Soul Survivor has done a huge amount to open people's eyes to the possibilities of worship, to inspire them and to help them towards a real encounter with God. But it has also promoted a model of worship as pop concert, as a

---

[4] Matt Redman, 'When the music fades', SOF 1113, 1997.

huge entertainment. The danger of worship being too emotionally led, too much of an entertainment, is that it relies very much on the occasion. When the atmosphere and emotion become the driving force of worship, then what happens when they are removed? This is the cause of the 'post-Big Top' syndrome that affects so many Christians every spring. That time in the Big Top, that time in the main meeting, *that* was worship. But the worship in our church? Well, let's just say it's not half so entertaining.

Part of the problem lies in the fact that we have relied too much on the event and not enough on the substance. Please believe me, I am not knocking these big events. Indeed, hearing God speak to me at a main meeting at Spring Harvest changed my life. I will be for ever grateful for that. But we always have to keep checking that, at these big events, people are worshipping God and not just enjoying the band.

In this struggle, what we sing becomes very important. You can't easily take away the musicianship and atmosphere of Soul Survivor and transpose it to the 15-strong church of St Kylie's that you usually attend. Great musicianship is hard to replicate. But wherever you are, and however many of you are worshipping, you can still think about the words. Great words do not require a great band; they only require a receptive spirit and an inquiring mind.

If the words are inadequate to start with, then the post-Big Top feeling will be even more of a let-down. Great musicianship can, indeed, paper over the cracks. In churches with large congregations, with better musicians, in the Big Top at Spring Harvest, the banalities of the lyrics are not so evident – we can revel in the musicianship and allow it to sweep us away. But take away the big band and it's like something is missing. Take away the impressive backing or the highly-skilled worship band and you are often left with nothing more than a trite song, a collection of platitudes. So our times of worship seem so bland, so un-nourishing. 'What's happened?' we wonder. 'The worship in the Big Top was so great. What's changed?' What has changed is that there is no longer any safety net. There are no longer talented artists and a 38-piece orchestra to make the whole thing sound great. There is just Mrs Jenkins on the piano and the vicar clapping resolutely out of time.

You can get away with bad lyrics when there's a rock-stadium atmosphere. But in the cold light of day, the super-ficiality of the songs is only too evident. What nourished us was the band, the atmosphere, the emotion of the occasion; not the lyrics of the song.

From writer to rock star

One further fall-out from the change to the pop aesthetic. We are seeing a generation of 'worship leaders' who have the profile of rock stars. They have high-profile personas. Their worship songs are sold in the form of CD albums. They appear on the cover looking moody/arty/holy/joyful as appropriate. We have worship songs crafted on pop songs. We have worship times played like rock concerts. We have focused all the creativity into one figure; a singer-songwriter. What's more natural than that they should become a rock star themselves?

I am not saying they deliberately cultivate this; in fact I should imagine that many of them feel deeply uneasy about such a development. But a worship culture modelled on the pop world demands its pop stars, whether they like it or not.

I am not knocking them for selling CDs. And I'm not falling into the old trap of knocking the Christian subculture. Young people need Christian artists to inspire them and to entertain them. I don't mind the Christian subculture; it helps me to make a living. But there is something profoundly wrong with a model of worship as performance. There is something very unsettling about the way that the focus can move so easily from the God we are worshipping to the people leading the worship. In some cases this manifests itself by people choosing which conference or meeting to go to, depending on who is leading the worship.

Worship leaders – like any other kind of Christian leader – are servants. They are not there to be waited on, but to wait on others; to lead them into a place of worship. And we serve them best by helping them to worship in spirit and in truth.

I am not saying that any of them have deliberately cultivated this. What I am saying is that if you play pop songs, in a pop-concert atmosphere, to people who are addicted to the emotional rush, then you will be treated like a kind of rock star because that's what you are.

The only way out of it is to change the way we view worship, to change the way that we interact with the people in the congregation. To get the people out there to think about what they are doing and to take worship seriously.

By this I don't mean that we have to be serious and po-faced about it. I don't mean we should go back to the days when everyone in church seemed to dress in grey and when the highest expression of joy was a quick chorus of 'This little light of mine'.[5] I mean that even our joy has to be grounded in a deep and sincere understanding of the nature of God.

---

[5] I don't have any details of this one – think it's 'traditional'!

Worship – joyful worship – should not be a mindless rave style blow-out. We are celebrating God, not partying the night away. There is a purpose to proceedings. There is meaning not madness.

We should dare to do what most pop performers can never dream of doing: getting our audience to think.

If that means stopping being a rock star for a moment, then so be it. If that means letting someone else write the lyrics to our latest masterpiece, then that's fine. If that means replacing pop-style superficiality with poem-like substance, then let's go for it.

Key points

- The worship song is modelled on the pop song rather than the poem; this leads to a downgrading of the importance of the lyric.

- Many worship song writers have taken on the singer-songwriter model; this has led to talented lyricists being left without an outlet for their gifts.

- This emphasis on emotion has led to an increasingly self-centred mode of worship. Instead we should be focusing on Jesus – the object of our worship.

- Too much worship is based on the pop concert; this has led to an emphasis on emotion and difficulties in encouraging effective worship in churches which cannot meet the musical challenges.

- Worship leaders are being pushed into the role of rock stars. But worship leaders are servants.

Key questions

- When you lead worship, do you concentrate on stirring the emotions?

- What role do emotions play in worship?

- How can we avoid over-emotionalism while at the same time avoiding an over-cerebral approach?

- Pop songs aim to capture emotions rather than intellect. Do you agree?

- How can worship leaders avoid becoming rock stars?

- How can you serve people through worship leading?

Kevin Molecule
27a Cinderpile Crescent
Stoke Poges

Mr Dave Davey
Songs of Dwellingness Ministries
Briglimpton
SUSSEX

Hi Dave,

Glad to hear that the sales team liked the new
stuff. I think I'm really going places now.
Doing a lot of work on my piano and guitar
technique and it's really starting to pay off.

You asked about my influences – in music
and words. I've listed all the music ones on
a sheet for you. When it comes to the words,
well, I don't really have any influences
– other than the Bible of course! It's more
a thing about inspiration, isn't it? I mean,
David didn't have any manuals or influences
when he wrote all those psalms did he? No, he
just wrote from the heart. And that's what I
try to do.

Sometimes people don't understand this. Like
with the following song, which God gave me the
other day during my lunch break. I hardly had
to rewrite a line. What a blessing! Here it is.

I am entering the land yet again
To see your face veiled in majesty
Standing in my garments of righteousness
Holy wind of God, blow on me.
I come before you now,

Standing humbly on my knees;
I will trust in you
You're my rock in stormy seas
Refine me like the potter and his clay,
Like the deer pants for the water,
I want you to 'light the fire again'.
I'm doing what I oughter.

I'm sure you can see the anointing in that song! But when I played it before the band some of them started to pick holes in it. Brian said that if God was veiled in majesty then how could I see his face? And if the sea was stormy then wouldn't I be safer in a harbour than on a rock? And then Celia said, like, how could you stand on your knees? And if the deer was thirsty then why was he asking God to relight his fire?

And then even Josh got in on the act. He said that the rhyme at the end wasn't any good. And I'm sure that during the bit about the wind of God I heard him snigger. But I didn't say anything, because I think he's still dealing with the firework incident. And after all, he is a drummer, so you have to make allowances.

But it's a bit depressing. It's like I present them with this prophetic outpouring and all they do is pick it to pieces! Sometimes I think these people don't understand inspiration at all. Still, all great artists suffer don't they?

With deep anointing,

Kevin Molecule
Worship Leader

As long as you're sincere: or
The importance of technique

Heart not art

I once wrote a book called *In Search of the World's Worst Writers* – devoted to writers of truly bad literature. One of the things which characterised a truly bad writer was that they believed that heart was more important than art. As long as your intentions were good, as long as your heart was in the right place, then the words didn't matter so much.

For example, in 1912, the loss of the *Titanic* led to an outpouring of poetic grief. Throughout the nation, people rushed to put their thoughts into print and the best of these poems were captured in a book: *Poetical Tributes on the Loss of the Titanic*. The foreword to the book was written by Charles F. Forshaw LLD who tried his best to prepare the reader for some of the poems that follow:

> The reader's indulgence is claimed for any imperfections due to accidents of birth or station. Some of the finest ideas are in many cases contained in verses of faulty construction, diction or metre, whilst poems unimpeachable in those respects are often deficient in spirit or originality.

Never mind the quality, he's saying, never mind the lack of technique. At least they're sincere. It's summed up by another 'entertainingly bad' writer, Ella Wheeler Wilcox who wrote:

> And therefore I say again, though I am art's one true lover,
> That it is not art, but heart, which wins the wide world
> over.[1]

This is the traditional argument of the bad poet. It's the thought that counts; what really matters is the sincerity of the writer; the *heart*.

Well, of course heart does matter. As we have seen – and as I hope to demonstrate when we come to look at a classic example – great worship songs are born out of deep reflection, out, indeed, of great worship. Without a deep experience of God, you cannot hope to lead others into worship. So godliness is vital for any aspiring worship song writer. You cannot inspire people unless you are inspired. You cannot offer people water from an empty well.

But godliness alone is not enough. It has to be married to other skills. Good intentions are no replacement for good technique. You might be a saint. You might have the most fantastic prayer life. You might be a prophet on a par with Elijah. But you still have to work at your craft. You have to work at your technique. The poet Tennyson wrote:

> A good hymn is the most difficult thing in the world to write.[2]

When a great poet says that, you've got to take it seriously. So this chapter is about technique. It's about the way we approach our craft and the need to do it right.

---

[1] Both above quotes are from Nick Page's *In Search of the World's Worst Writers* (London: HarperCollins, 2000), pp. 38, 241–2.
[2] Hallam Tennyson, *Tennyson: A Memoir* (London: Macmillan & Co, 1899), p. 37.

Let's hear it for Bezalel

I remember years ago meeting a Christian drama group who proudly told me, 'We spend more time praying than we do rehearsing.' And you know what? It showed. They might have been the most godly drama group in the entire world. They might rush straight out of their performance to heal the sick and raise the dead. But they weren't very good actors.

Any artist has to work hard at their technique. In relation to Christian service, some people find this hard to deal with. Whenever we start to talk about technique in reference to preaching or worship, people start to feel uneasy. Any talk of technique is 'worldly'. Surely it's not about technique? Surely it's about staying close to God, listening to him; doing what he wants? The world uses 'techniques'; Christians rely on inspiration.

To which the short answer is: no they don't.[3] Christians rely in each and every service on a wide range of techniques to convey their message. Any musician will tell you, for example, that you have to practise. Musicians rely on technique; the right way of doing things, the most effective way to get things done. Preachers have technique; and the best preachers have the best technique. Technique, according to the Oxford English Dictionary, means: 'mechanical skill in art, a means of achieving one's purpose, esp. skilfully, a manner of artistic execution in music, painting, etc.'

There's nothing sinister about any of this. Technique doesn't remove the need for prayerfulness, for Bible study or for contemplation. Technique is what can help those disciplines bear fruit.

---

[3] Actually there's a shorter answer than that. But I'm too polite to use it.

In the Bible there are lots of examples of literary technique at work. The book of Lamentations, for instance, is written mainly in the form of an acrostic; a poetic form where each line begins with a successive letter of the Hebrew alphabet. It's a very formal, difficult literary device, needing a great deal of work on the part of the writer to achieve the effect he wanted. Similarly, many psalms are crafted using specific Hebrew poetic techniques. That doesn't undermine their inspirational nature or their power to move us. It just means that the writers worked hard at what they had to say. They wanted to get it right.

What matters is that we employ the technique, we don't rely on it. Our technical skill, our craftsmanship, is put at the service of God. It's a channel for the Holy Spirit, not a replacement for the Holy Spirit.

We see this clearly in the Bible, in the story of Bezalel. Bezalel is the archetypal Spirit-filled craftsman. Here's how the Bible describes him:

> The LORD said to Moses: I have chosen Bezalel from the Judah tribe to make the sacred tent and its furnishings. Not only have I filled him with my Spirit, but I have given him wisdom and made him a skilled craftsman who can create objects of art with gold, silver, bronze, stone, and wood.
>
> (Ex. 31:1-5, CEV)

There are three things that spring out from this passage. First, Bezalel was a *skilled* craftsman. He knew his technique. He knew how to select the wood, plane it smooth, cut it precisely. He knew how to melt and hammer gold and silver. He knew how to carve stone. He was an artist. He'd spent years, probably, learning his craft, preparing, although he couldn't have known it, for the greatest commission of his life, that moment when God rang him up and said, 'Hi there. Like your work. Got a job for you ...'

Second, Bezalel *thought and reflected* on his art. God gave him wisdom. In the Bible, wisdom is a prized quality, one that people are encouraged to pursue. It comes as a gift from God, both directly and through other people. Proverbs encourages us to pass on wisdom, to sharpen each other as 'iron sharpens iron'.[4] This is a man who has thought long and hard about his craft and about its use; who has discussed his work with others and learnt from them. In Exodus 36:1, we discover that Bezalel was leading a team of craftsmen-artists, including Oholiab and people 'to whom the LORD has given skill and ability' (NIV).

Third, and most crucially, he's guided by God. He's a *Spirit-filled* artist. His craftsmanship and skill were set to work on God's plans. He allowed his hands to be steered by the Lord. Indeed, in Bible terms, his craftsmanship and skill were seen as evidence of the Spirit of God. The fact that he could do all these things, the fact that he had pondered and considered and gained wisdom – all these things show that Bezalel was a man open to God's Spirit.

He had 'paid his dues'. He had studied his craft and mastered it. He was open to God's direction. That's why he was given the task of making some of the most important and powerful objects in history; the ark of the covenant, the tabernacle and all its furnishings. The ark of the covenant was a box containing the most powerful truth on earth. The ark – an old English word which just means 'box' or 'chest' – had to be done right, because the contents were powerful; God's holiness is a dangerous substance. Bezalel had studied long and hard. He'd learnt about and reflected

---

[4] Prov. 27:17.

on his craft. He was a Spirit-filled man. That's why God chose him for the job.

At the risk of pushing the analogy too far, every Christian artist, every worship song writer is a kind of mini-Bezalel. We're all trying to fashion containers for God's truth. That truth is powerful, even dangerous. That truth can inspire, protect, comfort and amaze. So, like Bezalel, we should study our craft, learn all we can, listen to what God wants; and then set to work.

Technique is hard work

Of course inspiration matters. As we've seen in the story of Bezalel, it was God's inspiration that guided his hand, that made the ark what it was. But sometimes, 'inspiration' can be used as an excuse; a way of avoiding hard work. I've heard people say that 'this came to me so quickly, I must have been inspired'. And most of the time I look at their work and think, 'no, you were just in a hurry'. But it's hard to say that to someone. If people claim that a song has been 'given to them by God' it becomes very hard to criticise it. You can't easily argue with someone who claims divine revelation.

The truth is, I think, that inspiration can only take you so far. Inspiration is the fuel that powers the car; but you still have to pass your test. You still have to know how to drive. When it comes to writing words, inspiration is important, but other things come into play as well. Things like vocabulary and rhyme schemes and imagination and invention. The more disciplined you are about your writing, the better your song will be and the more faithfully you will serve the inspiration behind that song.

Most worship writers have probably never had any training in words – certainly not as much as they have with music. They might spend hours at the piano or playing the guitar. But they probably don't sit down and say, 'I'm going to practise my words today.' How many, I wonder, ever read poetry or listen to song lyrics with the sole aim of understanding how the thing works? How many have ever had any training in lyric writing or poetry? I've run workshops for dramatists and writers – but never one for worship song writers. I'm aware that there are courses springing up for worship leaders and song writers at various colleges around the country. I very much hope that they spend as much time looking at the words as they do at the music.

Frankly, I don't get the impression that many song writers study the work of previous generations. They might play the songs or hymns during services or events, but they don't sit down and really examine them; take them apart and see what makes them tick.

Nor am I very sure that they push themselves hard enough. The great lyricist Stephen Sondheim fills an entire notebook with thoughts and ideas that are crafted into one song. An *entire notebook* for each song. In all honesty, you could take all thoughts and ideas behind many worship songs and fit them onto the back of a postcard.

Great lyric writing is a gift. But like all gifts, it can be sharpened and honed. You can get better at it. I don't want to turn worship song writing into some academic exercise, like those screenwriting courses where screenplays are constructed by the manual; the writing equivalent of painting by numbers, but I do want worship song writers to examine their technique and to learn from others.

Doo dee doo dee doo

Sometimes the problem is simple: the words just don't make sense. It's not just the increasing number of 'pop style' choruses (kind of, dah-dah, la-la).[5] There's a place for spontaneous la-la-la-ing in worship, I suppose. (Although I can't help feeling that if you have to write it down then some of the spontaneity might go out of it.)

It's that sometimes, taken as a whole, the lines just don't make sense. They may have had a meaning to those who wrote them (I *hope* they had a meaning to those who wrote them) but somewhere along the way that meaning was quietly kidnapped, dragged off and bludgeoned to death by poor syntax, confusing grammar and obscure imagery.

Often the problem is that personal reflection, study or experience has just been poured straight into a song, without much thought for those who have to sing it. For example, a song like 'You have taken the precious'[6] uses imagery which I believe you can only understand if you have taken a course in Old Testament agriculture. It talks about harvests and ploughmen and threshing floors – images which even most modern farmers would struggle to comprehend. I think the problem here is that the song is simply too personal to be understood. It was obviously the result of deep personal reflection, but, in my opinion, the writers have failed to explain their meaning to their audience. Worship songs are not solely vehicles for personal expression, they're invitations to corporate worship. If you want to write stuff that only you can understand then keep a diary, otherwise you have to cut the rest of us some slack; you have to help us understand.

---

[5] Obviously the distinction between 'dah-dah' and 'la-la' is crucial.
[6] Kevin Prosch and Tom Davis, 'You have taken the precious', SOF 1138, 1991. Based on Amos 9:13 and Is. 55:1; 61:3. Not to mention Hag. 2:6, 7; Rom. 8:22; 1 Cor. 1:27 and Rev. 22:17.

The cliché

As the old joke goes, 'I avoid clichés like the plague.'

A cliché is any tired, over-used or oft-repeated phrase. In worship songs the clichés tend to come from the Bible. We have a surfeit of lambs, armour, panting deer and knees bowing and other such well-worn biblical phrases, which I will discuss in the next chapter. But there are other clichés from popular music or literature which also crop up regularly. Our hearts are often on fire. If we want to praise God's creation it's generally the mountains that do it for us, or possibly the trees. Justice always 'flows' and always like a 'river'. We're rescued from dungeons or chains. Darkness covers the land. God roars like a lion or is as solid as a rock.

All of this is true, but that's what a cliché is; it's something that is true, but which has lost its power to communicate because it has been over-used. Familiarity has bred, if not contempt, then apathy. We can't see things afresh because we've heard it all before.

A cliché is lazy writing. I don't care if it comes from the Bible or not. I don't care if it's a classic image of God. All I care about is that the moment I see it I've stopped thinking about things. It's not a new way of seeing things.

And it doesn't have to be that way. Creation songs, for example, don't have to bang on about the same old bits of scenery that we've all heard about before. Why fill your creation songs with mountains and trees and bits from the Bible? Haven't we discovered new things about this world which lead us to praise? Has David Attenborough spent his whole life in vain? A song like 'God is great' uses modern, relevant and beautiful images to bring nature before us.[7] You have to think as you sing; and when you think you see

---

[7] Graham Kendrick/Steve Thompson, 'God is Great', SOF 730, 1993.

the pictures in your mind; and when you see the pictures in your mind, you praise the Being who made the rainforest and the mist and those discordant, outrageous creatures.

And Matt Redman's song 'Show me the way of the cross'[8] breaks out of clichéd images to challenge us with the way we have turned the cross of Christ into a familiar, comfortable lifestyle. This is a brilliant song which is not, I think, as well known as it should be. Perhaps because it's too surprising, too challenging; singing those lines about our 'comfortable crosses' breaks us out of clichéd imagery and into very sharp, very personal, very uncomfortable reflection.

It is part of the worship song writer's job to startle and stimulate; to create new pictures and new images in our minds. Clichés cannot do this. They are tired; they are lazy. Avoid them like the _____ (fill in your own new, exciting avoidance-based metaphor here).

Mixed metaphors

Use metaphors please. But use them properly. Make them count. Mix your metaphors and you mix your meanings. A mixed metaphor will simply weaken the power and meaning of your song. Take Kevin's line:

> Refine me like the potter and his clay.[9]

There are two metaphors going on here, the fire that purifies metal and the potter who moulds the clay. You can't put the two together. Of course, you say, Kevin's not a real example. But I could quote you others, where discordant images are welded together.

---

[8] Matt Redman, 'Show me the way of the cross', SOF 1000, 1996.

[9] Kevin Molecule, 'I am entering the land yet again', Deeply Anointed Ministries, 2004.

This might seem nit-picking. But words matter. Put them together in the wrong way, or in a muddle, and you sow confusion instead of shining a light ... oh, hang on, that's a mixed metaphor ...

Bad rhyme

I don't mind if you don't rhyme. In fact, I'd rather you didn't rhyme at all, if you can't do it well. It's not that I don't enjoy bad rhymes – one of my favourite poets is a man called James McIntyre, a Canadian who wrote mainly on the theme of cheese.

> When cows give milk from spring fodder
> You cannot make a good cheddar.
> The quality is often vile
> Of cheese that is made in April.[10]

Now that's bad rhyming bordering on genius. Sadly few people can aspire to McIntyre's depths. Mostly when the rhymes are bad in worship songs they just induce a wince. And everyone does it. Car crashes happen to the best of drivers. Here's Wordsworth showing that even genius has its off-days:

> This piteous news, so much it shocked her,
> She quite forgot to send the Doctor.[11]

You want a Christian example? OK, to prove that greats have feet of clay, there's a Graham Kendrick song which

---

[10] James McIntyre, 'Dairy Ode', quoted in Nick Page's *In Search of the World's Worst Writers*, p. 79.
[11] Wordsworth, 'The Idiot Boy', quoted in Nick Page's *In Search of the World's Worst Writers*, p. 191.

rhymes the word blaze with the word face.[12] Now I think GK is a great songwriter but that one isn't even *close*. It forces you into pronouncing the word face as if you are drunk.

This can be a legitimate poetic technique. It's called the 'imperfect rhyme' or 'oblique rhyme', where the rhyme is close but not exact. The trouble with this is that it's an OK rhyme for verses that we read on the page, but it's just annoying when you have to sing them. When you read it on the page, your eye takes in the shape of the words, your mind accepts the difference. Sing it out loud and at the top of your voice, however, and things become a little more apparent. Sung rhymes should, I think, aim to be perfect or exact rhymes. They are part of the rhythm and the cadence of the music. A perfect rhyme fits with the end of a musical phrase. An imperfect rhyme doesn't. It is too tentative, too uncertain, too, well, *imperfect*.

In a song like 'At the foot of the cross' for example, every other line is an imperfect rhyme. It's sort of an a b a b-minus rhyming scheme.[13] Throughout the song, the second and fourth lines just never quite make it into the same rhyming scheme. Obviously the writer has decided to do this as a conscious decision. This is a good song, with an important point to make, but the sheer number of imperfect rhymes makes the song seem tentative and uncertain. If you're going to use imperfect rhymes, use them sparingly. Personally – and I accept this may just be a personal preference – I think they work better in poetry than in worship singing.

---

[12] Actually, I've just noticed that the song from which this comes – 'Teach Me to Dance' – is credited to Graham Kendrick and Steve Thompson. Sort it out boys, will you?

[13] Tré Shephard, 'At the foot of the cross'.

I guess the rule is if you're going to rhyme, rhyme properly. If you're not going to rhyme don't tease us by occasionally doing so. Be consistent.

Variable syllables

And talking of being consistent ...

One thing we have to remember in writing worship songs: people will sing them. Now congregational singing, whether you're in a cathedral or in a converted warehouse, relies on a strong beat. It relies on a well-established pattern of notes that people can follow, that they can sing along to. And the words have to sit on top of those notes and follow the same lines.

So it's important to stick to your pattern and to make sure that the number of syllables in your verses doesn't alter from verse to verse. If the syllable count drops below the musical notes, or increases above them, then the singers have to cram in more syllables or extend them. For example, in the otherwise excellent song 'O give me a hearing heart O Lord', the fourth line of the first verse has nine syllables, while the fourth line of the second verse has seven syllables.[14] Now one or other of these lines is going to have to be rushed or stretched to fit the melody. They can't both be right.

Stretching the syllables or cramming more in is perfectly OK if you're the singer of the song. You know what's coming up, you've rehearsed it, you know where the adjustments have to be made. But congregations don't have that luxury. They have to stop thinking about the words and start thinking about how to fit the words in. And that means that the worship will be interrupted.

---

[14] Phil Lawson Johnston, 'O give me a hearing heart O Lord', 1987.

Of course, it happens in pop songs all the time. Some of the greatest lyricists change the scansion of their songs. Joni Mitchell, for example. But Joni Mitchell isn't inviting her audience to sing along with her. She's not writing songs for congregational singing but for performance. And, whether they like it or not, worship song writers are writing songs for other people to sing. Which means that the songs should aim to be 'singable'.

Mucking about with the syllable count might serve the writer's need to get across what they want to say, but it's not serving the needs of the congregation.

Think of football chants. Football chants nearly always rhyme and they always fit the notes of the songs. Why? Because that's the way people work. Cramming in extra syllables is something that performers do, not something that worship leaders should do.

The unintentional meaning

Sometimes I wonder what goes through the minds of the people who write the worship songs. I can only assume that they have lost all touch with the non-Christian world. Of course, worship songs are written for Christians, but maybe sometimes we ought to stop and think, 'what would a non-Christian make of this?' That is not a reason, of course, for necessarily toning down or changing what we have to write; we write what we believe we are called to write. But it might make us think twice. It might make us look for alternative phrasing where possible.

Now, 'To the pure, all things are pure' (Titus 1:15a, NIV). But, as a friend of mine is fond of saying, to the puerile all is puerile. So best not to give those kind of people – like me – more ammunition than we need, because when you do you scupper all chance of true worship occurring. Even if we resist the urge to snigger, we'll be *concentrating* on resisting the urge to snigger. And you can't worship effectively when you're trying not to laugh.

For example, some years ago I was on the board of a fairly large Christian charity. At one of our annual conferences I was at the end of one row, while the Chief Executive was at the other end of the seats. We began, as is obligatory in all Christian meetings, with a time of worship. The first chords struck up and I gazed in expectancy at the overhead projector screen. Now, I have to admit my mind is slightly hazy on the details, but I seem to recall that the writer of the song expressed a desire to feel the wind of the Lord upon their face. I can't recall precisely because I only looked at it for a moment before collapsing into a shameful fit of giggling.

Believe me, I tried everything. I squeezed my hands together until they went numb. I tried to think of deeply unfunny things: funerals, disasters, the M25. But then I looked along the row to see my friend – the Chief Executive of this important Christian organisation – weeping with repressed laughter. That was it. I was gone. I had to leave the room quickly and hope that people thought I was repenting.

I'm not proud of this, but I'm not terribly ashamed of it either. It was just a human reaction. And if the song had been tested with anyone other than a group of 'saints', it might have been written differently.

Sometimes this happens because words change their meaning over time. The great Christian mystical poet Henry Vaughan wrote a poem which includes the line,

How bright a prospect is a bright backside![15]

---

[15] Quoted in D.B. Wyndham-Lewis and C.B. Lee (ed.), *The Stuffed Owl* (London: J.M. Dent, 1935), p. 1.

While I remember as a youngster singing a hymn which included the memorable line,

> Here I raise my Ebenezer.[16]

I'm not sure what that means, but please, don't try it at home.

Give them time

Avoiding these kinds of faults takes time and discipline. So let your work develop. Give it time to grow and to change. Don't finish a lyric and rush into church or into the studio. Revisit it. Let the words have space to breathe and mature.

Sometimes we rush into these things – or we leave the whole thing far too late. I have to admit that I am very guilty of this. As a professional hack I'm always working up to deadlines – and often past deadlines, delivering things at the last minute, getting it done by the skin of my teeth. This is not the way to create good, lasting work.

Instead the way is to spend time on it. Think it through. Look at it again and again. Try out different versions and different ideas. And it goes without saying that you should lay your lyrics before the Lord. He, above all, will know when something has been ill thought out or rushed. Pray them through. Give time to them. That way you will be able not only to correct the faults but also to enhance the virtues of your work.

---

[16] From the hymn 'Come, thou fount of every blessing' written by Robert Robinson who died in 1795. It's actually based on 1 Sam. 7: 12, where the word Ebenezer means 'Thus far has the LORD helped us' (NIV). But then you knew that ...

How do we learn?

The kind of technical faults I've listed above are pretty easy to spot with a little practice. But there are other aspects of technique which are harder to learn. Particularly things like song-structure and imagery. These are skills which are only developed over time and through practice. Nevertheless, there are ways in which we can address these issues; the main way being to examine the work of other writers and learn from them.

And, believe me, we should never tire of learning. As my wife says, the difference between an amateur and a professional is that a professional never stops learning. If by a professional worship song writer we mean one who takes their craft seriously and who wants to push it as far as it can go, then we should learn all we can, whenever we can.

Otherwise all we'll ever be is amateurs, dabbling at the edges, and never seeing how far we can swim.

Learn from others (part one): current writers

The most fundamental thing in improving your technique is to listen to and learn from others you admire. Talk to other worship song writers about their craft. Share ideas and inspiration. Examine their work and try to understand how they do it.

Learning from the experts means sitting down with a lyric and taking it to pieces. How does the language work? Why are the images so potent? What's the rhyme scheme and structure? Look at how the words 'sit' on the tune and how they make it easy to sing. Examine the phrasing. Great songs will always seem natural when they are sung; a bad lyric always seem clumsy and forced.

Of course you can take your lyrics from anywhere. I'd advise a pretty wide approach. Look at the work of songwriters in a wide variety of different disciplines.

There is nothing wrong in this, providing you don't just set out to mimic them. Imitation may be the sincerest form of flattery, but it's the lousiest form of lyric writing. Whenever a great worship song comes along, you tend to see a flurry of smaller ones following in its wake, using almost identical imagery and ideas.

That's not really learning, though. The way to learn is to identify what is special about that song, and then see if you can apply that to an entirely different subject. For example, a song like 'Meekness and majesty'[17] relies upon a strong structure and constant juxtaposition of ideas. The core theme of the song is the incarnation of God in Christ and the song embodies this not only in what the words say, but in the way that they're put together. Everything in this song is designed to reinforce the central message that Jesus was both man and God. In later verses this feeling of duality is reinforced and developed by a series of paradoxes; the idea of conquering through sacrifice, of an indestructible love in a frail body. This is a song of comparisons. It always combines or contrasts two ideas. The result is a fantastic lyric, where the structure echoes the message.

Now the temptation here would be to go out and write a song full of contrasting qualities and juxtaposed statements called 'Beauty and Ugliness'. As I said, that's not really learning; copying really doesn't teach you much.

No, to learn from this song, take it apart, see how it works and then look at how you can apply those tech-niques in your own song. Can you use juxtaposed ideas and contrasts like this? Can you make people think by presenting them

---

[17] Graham Kendrick, SOF 360.

with a paradox? Most of all, can you embody the theme of
your song in the structure of your lyric?

Learning from others (part two): the classics

The literary critic Cyril Connelly once wrote a book called
Enemies of Promise[18] in which he investigated whether or
not it was possible to write a book that would 'last ten
years'. It's a question that maybe worship song writers
should aim to address. Will this song last ten years?
Will it last ten months? Should our aim not be to create
something that will last as long as possible? In the end,
maybe it's not possible to guarantee this; you can't just
press the 'Make this song a classic' button on your word
processor. But maybe we can learn what it is that makes
songs last.

At the beginning of this book, I took a quick look at the
history of hymn-writing and worship song writing over
the past 300 or so years. We saw how the rise of hymn-
writing led to a huge number being in circulation, and how
through a process of 'hymnological Darwinism', only the
fittest have survived. So one of the best ways to learn about
worship song writing is to look at one of the survivors.
After all, if they're still being sung hundreds of years later,
they must have done something right.

Let's look at one of the most famous hymn lyrics of
them all . . .

Amazing Grace
This is probably the best-known hymn, ever. Indeed, its
very familiarity can blind us to just how good a piece of
work it is.

---

[18] See Cyril Connolly, *Enemies of Promise* (London: Penguin Modern
Classics, 1961), p. 16.

It was written by John Newton, a pastor in Olney, Buckinghamshire, was originally entitled 'Faith's Review and Expectation' and was based on 1 Chronicles 17:16, 17.

> David went into the tent he had set up for the sacred chest. He sat there and prayed: LORD God, my family and I don't deserve what you have already done for us, and yet you have promised to do even more for my descendants. You are treating me as if I am a very important person.
>
> (1 Chron. 17:16, 17, CEV)

It was originally written as a poem and published in a book, *Olney Hymns*, in 1788. Newton didn't write the tune; indeed, it seems to have had several different tunes applied to it, before finally settling comfortably into the one we all know in *Virginia Harmony*, an American hymnal from 1831. The tune is, apparently, called 'New Britain' and is believed to be Scottish or Irish in origin. Which is probably why it works so well with the bagpipes. (Or not. Depending on what you think of bagpipes. Personally I think that you should be careful of any instrument which makes it sound like you are torturing a heifer, but there you go.)

Here's the whole thing. Enjoy.

> Amazing grace! (how sweet the sound)
> That sav'd a wretch like me!
> I once was lost, but now am found,
> Was blind, but now I see.
>
> 'Twas grace that taught my heart to fear,
> And grace my fears reliev'd;
> How precious did that grace appear,
> The hour I first believ'd!
>
> Thro' many dangers, toils and snares,
> I have already come;
> 'Tis grace has brought me safe thus far,
> And grace will lead me home.

The Lord has promis'd good to me,
His word my hope secures;
He will my shield and portion be,
As long as life endures.

Yes, when this flesh and heart shall fail,
And mortal life shall cease;
I shall possess, within the veil,
A life of joy and peace.

The earth shall soon dissolve like snow,
The sun forbear to shine;
But God, who call'd me here below,
Will be forever mine.[19]

OK. By now you're either in awe of this song, or bored by
having to read it again, or wondering whether all this is
really here because I'm a closet hymn-fascist and despite
my protestations, I'm about to condemn any music made
after about 1890 as depraved and possibly satanic. But
bear with me, what we're interested in here is technique.
We're trying to find out what it is about this hymn that
has enabled it to last for so long.

First, a general point: this is a hymn that springs from
a deep, personal experience. Newton had been a big-time

---

[19] John Newton, 1725–1807. There's often a final verse added which
runs,

> When we've been there ten thousand years,
> Bright shining as the sun,
> We've no less days to sing God's praise
> Than when we'd first begun.

But this is not actually by Newton. It's from a hymn called 'Jerusalem,
My Happy Home' and was first added to the hymn in the novel
Uncle Tom's Cabin by Harriet Beecher Stowe. In the novel, the point
is that the singer, Uncle Tom, has got his hymn lyrics muddled. But
somehow it seems to have stuck.

sinner. After years of drinking and debauchery he became captain of a slave ship, before finally being converted by God and ending up a pastor of a church. So he knew what it was to receive forgiveness. He knew what it was to face danger and toil and to come safely home. To him, God's grace really was amazing, and this feeling of astonishment at the depth of God's love springs out from all the verses of this poem. This is a song born from real-life experience of a real-life God.

Christopher Driver called hymns 'a poetic response to experience'.[20] Our worship songs should be poetic responses to our experiences of God. They should spring from real encounters. They should not be rehashes of other people's experiences or rewrites of other lyrics. Newton had a deep experience of God, and through that he was able to bring others into a similar experience.

And Newton's personality shines through here. In truth, when he's preaching, when he's not talking directly from his own experiences, Newton's hymns are quite boring. But when he draws on his own life – his sin, his years of rebellion – then there is life and energy and power. Here we can picture the sailor lost at sea, the slave trader drifting and lost, but led home by the most amazing thing in the world.

And it is very much set in 'the world'. It's a physical experience. Newton has been saved. His sight has been restored. He has been brought home. It is this mix of ordinary, physical images – the dangers of the world here below and the goodness of the God above – with the marvellous, amazing grace that makes the hymn so powerful.

---

[20] Christopher Driver, 'Poetry and Hymns', *Congregational Quarterly*, 25 (1957), pp. 333–40.

Newton uses simple language throughout. Of course, to our eyes some of it seems a bit antiquated now, but that's because we're not living in the eighteenth century.[21] What's interesting is not that some of it sounds dated, but that so much of it still communicates so well. Because Newton knew he was talking to uneducated people, he kept his language and images relevant. This simple language and imagery gives the song a lot of pace and impact. There are only two words in this song longer than two syllables, and one of those is 'Amazing'. Everything else is two syllables or less; this means that the song has pace. You're always moving on to the next word, moving through the song, moving forward, learning something new. It also means that the lyrics sit perfectly on the melody.

This simplicity of language is typical of Newton, who prided himself on his simple language and his ability to talk about Jesus to people from all backgrounds.

> I am not conscious of having written a single line with an intention, either to flatter, or to offend any party or person upon earth. I have simply declared my own views and feelings, as I might have done if I had composed hymns in some of the newly-discovered islands in the South Sea, where no person had any knowledge of the name of Jesus but myself.[22]

Newton used many ordinary images as themes for his hymns, including magnets, bees, thawing ice and the sea.[23] He also used contemporary events as a basis for his hymns, like the eclipse of the moon in 1776, which he

---

[21] Well, most of us aren't, anyway. I know a few people who are medieval, but that's mainly a matter of personal hygiene.

[22] John Newton and William Cowper, *Olney Hymns*, p. ix.

[23] J.R. Watson, *The English Hymn*, p. 287.

used as the basis for a meditation on Christ's experience in Gethsemane, where the sins of the world deprived Christ of 'the light of God'.

Let's have a look at it verse by verse.

> Amazing grace! (how sweet the sound)
> That sav'd a wretch like me!
> I once was lost, but now am found,
> Was blind, but now I see.

The poem uses a simple rhyming scheme: a b a b.[24] It's a classic; easy, memorable, natural. But it gives a real sense of solidity and significance to the verses. Each verse has a certainty to it, backed up by the strength of this scheme. Rhyme schemes can do so much more than just shape the poem, they can affect the tone. This is a certain, strong poem, enhanced by a certain, strong rhythm and rhyme scheme.

And it's such a great start! Newton was a master at starting and finishing his lines to guarantee maximum impact. The theme of his song is summed up in the opening two words: they sum up what his message is; the rest of the song goes on to expound and explain.

Note also that the metaphors are rigorously enforced; he is lost, he is found; he is blind, he sees. Each metaphor is applied with logic. He doesn't say 'I was blind, but now am found.' We're not at home to Mr Mixed Metaphor, thank you.

> 'Twas grace that taught my heart to fear,
> And grace my fears reliev'd;
> How precious did that grace appear,
> The hour I first believ'd!

---

[24] If you're not sure about rhyming schemes, they are explained on p. 117.

There's some important theology here. Newton is saying that it is God's grace which made him fearful; it was God who set him on the path that led to God. God's grace unsettles us, disturbs us until we find our rest in him. He awakens us to the problem and then provides the solution. This is deep stuff. Newton was set on the search by God and it was God who was the eventual outcome of his search. And when he commits himself, when he believes, he can see how valuable the gift is.

> Thro' many dangers, toils and snares,
> I have already come;
> 'Tis grace has brought me safe thus far,
> And grace will lead me home.

Ordinary pictures. Apart from that repeated 'theme' word – grace – there is no overt biblical language here. There is just the kind of language that ordinary agricultural-class labourers would have understood. The people who made up Newton's congregation in the small Buckinghamshire village knew about toil and danger. They knew about traps and snares.

> The Lord has promis'd good to me,
> His word my hope secures;
> He will my shield and portion be,
> As long as life endures.

The first two lines are a simple statement of fact: the Lord has promised to do good, and because he has said it, our hope is secure. In the second two lines 'shield' is self-explanatory, but 'portion' needs some explaining. In the eighteenth century it meant a part or share of an inheritance. So, the Lord is Newton's future inheritance as well as his current protection. It sounds biblical, but it wasn't; it was another everyday image.

> Yes, when this flesh and heart shall fail,
> And mortal life shall cease;
> I shall possess, within the veil,
> A life of joy and peace.

'Within the veil' is the only overt biblical reference in the entire hymn. It refers, of course, to the veil of the temple, as the curtain is translated in the King James version. Newton's readers would also have remembered Hebrews 6:19:

> Which hope we have as an anchor of the soul, both sure and steadfast, and which entereth into that within the veil.
>
> (KJV)

It's an archaic word now, but it was not so archaic for the singers and readers of this hymn when it was first published.

> The earth shall soon dissolve like snow,
> The sun forbear to shine;
> But God, who call'd me here below,
> Will be forever mine.

This verse is not familiar. We don't sing it much today, preferring the alternate, 'Uncle Tom' ending (see note 19). But I love this. Again, the language is simple and plain. It picks up on an image which would have been identifiable to Newton's audience: the image of the earth dissolving like melting snow is at once simple and powerful. But God's love doesn't melt. God, who has called us while we are still here 'below' on earth, will forever be ours. Now that's what I call amazing grace!

So, what do we learn from 'Amazing Grace'?

1. *It grows from a deep, personal and, above all, real experience of God*

   You want to write a great worship song? Draw deep on your personal experiences and then make them universal.

2. *It has a strong, simple structure*

   Simple rhyme schemes are matched with short, strong words. The result is energy and pace and a feeling of strength which mirrors the theme of the song.

3. *It uses ordinary language and images*

   Even today there is little of this hymn which is dated. Newton wrote for the people he knew, in the language they spoke.

4. *It has theological depth*

   You can grasp it at first reading; and then you can go deeper. This is a song born of contemplation; a song with a hinterland, where there is always more to explore.

All this, and a great tune. With or without the bagpipes.

Learn from others (part three): other people

I remember going into a major furniture store a few years ago and seeing a display about how they tested all their furniture. They had mechanised 'robots' that would open and close drawers, or simulate sitting on cushions. They would repeat this process thousands of times. That way they could be sure that the products would last.

How few of us test our words in anything like as much detail? How many people sit down and take their own lyrics to pieces? Most importantly, how many people ask others for feedback? Most often as writers we ask people for approval rather than constructive criticism. We look for people to accept our work, rather than improve it. We should be willing to hear from others. I mean we should get together with tried and tested friends and advisers who will critique our work in a positive and prayerful spirit.

It's not a question of listening to everyone's opinion. The idea that the customer is always right is ridiculous; and there are a great many people out there who wouldn't know a good lyric if it sat up and bit them. Which is why you need to develop a group of people whose judgement and taste you trust. A group of people who, frankly, know what they're talking about. I receive a lot of comments about the books I write; but the comments of certain people I will take a lot more notice of than others. These are the people I trust; the people I know who aren't interested in scoring points or 'having their say'; these are the people who want me to be the best artist I can.

Those kinds of people; the people who want you to be the best, most effective, most Spirit-filled and prophetic songwriter you can be, are gold dust. Treasure them. Learn from them. Listen to them. They have your best interest at heart.

Sometimes these people will pick up on problems with individual words or phrases. They'll help you to spot things that don't make sense. They'll challenge you with interpretations and meanings that you'd never considered. They'll have an understanding of the cultural context in which the song is to be sung. They'll simply help you to make your work better.

Key points

- Technique is important.

- Technique doesn't remove the need for prayerfulness, for Bible study or for contemplation. Technique is what can help those disciplines bear fruit.

- The more disciplined you are about your writing, the better your song will be and the more faithfully you will serve the inspiration behind that song.

- Check your words really mean what you think they mean.

- Avoid clichés and mixed metaphors.

- Keep your rhymes simple and strong.

- Be consistent, both with rhyming and with syllable count.

- Avoid words that have a double meaning – unless you want them to have a double meaning.

- Give time for your work to develop and to change.

- Keep learning, from current writers, classic works and from the people you trust.

Key questions

- Examine your own work. Is there stuff in there you would like to change? Why?

- Do you test your work with others? Is there a group of critical supporters to help you improve your songs?

- What lyric writers or hymn writers do you admire? Examine their work. Take it apart and see how it operates.

- Do you allow time in your writing? Or do you write your songs in a hurry?

- Do you spend time deliberately practising your words? Have you ever tried to write a lyric in a different format, just to see if you can?

Kevin Molecule
27a Cinderpile Crescent
Stoke Poges

Mr Dave Davey
Songs of Dwellingness Ministries
Briglimpton
SUSSEX

Hi Dave,

Thanks for your encouragement last time. I've
had to discipline some of the band, but I
think we're all marching together now.

   Which is good, because more and more I'm
convinced we're in a war. You know, it's a
battle, like Paul wrote about. I talked this
through with the band and they agreed with
me. (Except for Josh, who said that he didn't
know why Christians kept banging on about
fighting, when Paul wrote just as much about
agriculture or running. But who wants to
sing a song about running? Sometimes I really
don't think he's on the same wavelength as
the rest of us. But then, he is a drummer.)

   Anyway, here's my latest offering. As you
can see, I've been anointing myself with
the Bible lately. That's the thing about the
Bible: it's not just the word of God, it's a
great source of lyrics.

We will march into the land
With our two-edged sword in hand
But hold it by the handle 'cos it's safer.
I see the Lamb seated on the throne,

And his train,
Once again
Fills the temple with glory!

Terrible as an army with sandals,
We glorify in the Lamb once slain.
Refine me in your crucible for silver and for
  gold
And his train,
Of the slain
Once again
Fills the temple with glory!

He is the only one
Who ever bore our pain
So take now our grain offering
And his train
Of the slain
With their grain
In their pain
Once again
Fills the temple with glory!

With deep mercy,

Kevin Molecule
Worship Leader

Cracking the code: or
The problem of language

I recently read a hymn which had the lines,

> For Judah's Lion bursts his chains,
> Crushing the serpent's head.[1]

This reminds me of one of those cryptic messages that spies are supposed to give one another.

SCENE: Trafalgar Square. A man in a raincoat is standing reading *The Times* newspaper. Another man, in another raincoat, sidles up to him.

> Spy 1: Judah's lion has burst his chains.
> Spy 2: And crushed the serpent's head.
> Spy 1: Very good. Have you got the microfilm?

Sometimes it's like a code we're singing. It appears to be English. The words are all to be found in an English dictionary. But they don't make any sense.

---

[1] It begins,

> Ye choirs of new Jerusalem,
> your sweetest notes employ,
> the Paschal victory to hymn
> in strains of holy joy.

'Ye choirs of new Jerusalem', Robert Campbell, 1850, based on Fulbert of Chartre, eleventh century.

With hymns, of course, the reason is because we're singing words which were, in many cases, written hundreds of years ago. The language has moved on. Although some bits of the hymn have passed their 'understand-by' date, we still sing them because we like the tune, or because the rest of the hymn is great. Take, 'At the name of Jesus', which includes the lines,

> Humbled for a season,
> To receive a name
> From the lips of sinners
> Unto whom He came;
> Faithfully He bore it
> Spotless to the last,
> Brought it back victorious,
> When from death He passed.[2]

As a supporter of Watford Football Club I have, for many years, assumed this was some kind of prophecy about my team. After all, we have been humbled in many seasons, and have received many names – very few of which are printable here. Quite what this really means is beyond me. I assume that it's the name of 'Saviour', although the fact that Jesus bore it spotlessly makes it sound more like he got through a rugby match with a very, very clean shirt.

Sometimes we persist with these hymns because, well, it's traditional, isn't it? Christmas carols, for instance. Christmas wouldn't be Christmas without 'Hark! The herald-angels sing' or 'O come all ye faithful' or the syntactically confused 'We three kings of orient are'. Indeed 'Hark! The herald-angels sing' has some gloriously strange imagery. It was originally written by Charles Wesley and then edited and rewritten by George Whitfield and Martin

---

[2] Caroline M. Noel (died in 1877).

Madan. Which means that one of them is responsible for this:

> Hail, the Sun of Righteousness!
> Light and life to all He brings,
> Risen with healing in His wings[3]

This makes Jesus sound like a chicken with a medical degree.[4] In all the many years I have been enduring – sorry, enjoying – carol services no one has ever explained what this means. Maybe it's because those leading the services don't know what the words mean either.[5] But wouldn't it be good if, just one Christmas, someone explained these lines? Especially since the churches are so full of non-Christians at that time of year.

The fact that we don't know what this phrase means now is excusable, given that the song was originally written some time in the 1740s. But it's a bit strange to find exactly the same, obscure image used in a song written in 1994.[6]

Wesley, Whitfield and Madan at least had the excuse that they lived in the eighteenth century. But to carry on

---

[3] Originally written by Charles Wesley, 1707–88.

[4] Possibly, since he is bringing light, a luminous chicken with a medical degree.

[5] OK, I do know really. It comes from Mal. 4:2 which in the King James version runs:

> But unto you that fear my name shall the Sun of right-eousness arise with healing in his wings; and ye shall go forth, and grow up as calves of the stall.

'Wings' here means the rays of the sun. So Jesus rises like the sun and his rays heal us. You see? It's simple when you just go and consult about three versions of the Bible and the Oxford English Dictionary.

[6] Bob Baker, 'Well I thank you Lord', SOF 1096, 1994.

using an antique, confusing image, when absolutely no one uses the word 'wings' in that way (as in rays of the sun) any more seems just peculiar. Ah, but it's in the Bible. And not just the King James – it's in the NIV as well. So if it's in the Bible, then that's all right, isn't it?

It must be good, it's in the Bible

You'd be forgiven for thinking that the most important ability in writing worship songs is the ability to cut and paste verses from the Bible – simply rip out a chunk of Scripture and glue it into place. Never mind if the words don't fit, or the isolated verse doesn't make sense. It's the Bible! It must be holy. It's the religious version of the 'heart is more important than art' belief; the idea that if it's in the Bible it must be worth singing.

I love the Bible. I've spent large and unprofitable chunks of what I laughingly call my career in trying to encourage people to read the Bible. But when you read the Bible, or when you have it expounded to you in a sermon, the context and images can be explained. When you sing it there is no one providing any help.

First and foremost, this 'pick and mix' approach to Scripture makes a lot of assumptions about the level of people's Bible knowledge. Just because they've sat there for about a century or two, listening to the sermon, doesn't mean that they spot the references in your song to Lamentations or the clever way that you have likened the worshipping soul to the gazelles in Song of Songs. A song such as 'Take me past the outer courts', for example, requires the singer to have a pretty good knowledge of the layout of the temple in order to understand it, not to mention being able to spot the reference to Isaiah 6:6, 7.[7]

---

[7] Dave Browning, 'Take me past the outer courts', SOF 1012.

Otherwise it just reads like someone is giving me a load of directions to a place where I can get my mouth burnt. There are plenty of other examples that I could quote.

Second, I have to ask whether this approach sometimes compensates for a lack of application. It's hard to write a good song-lyric. Not everyone can do it. Far easier to stick a Bible verse in place than to come up with your own thoughts and words. This sounds very harsh, I know, but as the brief history of hymns and worship songs showed, the whole point of a worship song or hymn is that it is a reflection on Scripture. It's intended to teach, to encourage, to exhort – it's not just intended to repeat verbatim what's in the Bible. What's the point of doing that? Why not read it instead? At least that way you'd get the context.

And context matters. When I preach or teach I try to obey one of the fundamental rules of Bible exposition: set the verse in its context. But too many worship song writers don't do this. They grab verses at random, orphan them from the passage in which they were set, and present them without any explanation or development. Far from being a Bible-based approach, I would argue that this is profoundly unscriptural.

Sometimes it seems as though worship songs are in a competition to see exactly how many Bible verses they can cram in. Normally, the song writers list the references at the top of the page in the music books and an analysis of these reveals some interesting facts. In *Songs of Fellowship Book 2*, for example, there are quite a few songs with twelve Scripture references at the top, two with thirteen Scripture references and two with fourteen separate Scripture references! However, they're not the winner. No, there is one song that is more 'scripturised' than the rest. Yes, step forward SOF 1047 'These are the days of Elijah'[8] with a massive nineteen Scripture references![9]

The Dadaist poets used to practise random poetry; they would cut up a book into separate words or sentences, throw them in the air and paste them together how they landed. Sometimes I suspect that many worship song writers use a similar approach. Throw a load of scripture verses in the air, let them land and then just glue them together. It's fridge-magnet poetry; not really lyric-writing, just rearranging verses to fit.

Small wonder that the songs which draw most heavily on Scripture references are often the most fragmented and unfocused. The best songs make one main point and make it well. They might use lots of different images but those images are subservient to the purpose of the song. But it's difficult for a song to have one main purpose, when it's trying to embody at least ten different verses from widely different parts of the Bible.

The other effect of using either literal or thinly veiled Scripture verses is that it creates a kind of shield from criticism. As someone once said, if the dedication to your book is tragic enough it will almost guarantee you favourable reviews. In other words, if you put at the front of your book, 'To Little Maisie, with the fervent hope that one day she will recover the use of the lower limb on the right hand side of her body,' you won't get a single bad review. Whether or not that is true remains to be seen, but certainly there is a similar belief about using Bible verses in songs. They're like an anti-criticism insurance policy. How can we criticise songs with Bible

---

8 Robin Mark, 'These are the days of Elijah', SOF 1047, 1997.
9 What's interesting is that there are only sixteen lines in the song. That's an impressive 1.1875 references per line.

verses in? That would be like, well, like criticising the Bible itself.

Only it isn't. Because I'm not criticising the verses themselves, but the way they've been used. What I'm criticising is the habit of taking a verse out of context and presenting it without comment or explanation. I'm criticising the bad technique that 'squashes' many Bible verses uncomfortably into the melody like a tall man wearing a suit several sizes too small for him.

I'm criticising what is essentially a superficial approach. Earlier I talked about the need for deep songs, for songs that took an idea and really explored it. Songs crammed with Bible verses are not deep songs, because there is no exploration going on. There is just a random jumping about within Scripture. It's like a kind of scriptural Tourette's syndrome; we're just blurting out Bible verses. We don't mean anything by them; we just can't help ourselves.

It's old: it must be holy

Once upon a time I used to deal in second-hand books. (I stopped because I tended to buy all my own stock.) When people brought me books to value, they always said the same thing: 'It's leather-bound so we thought it must be worth something.' Never mind that the contents were dog-eared or mildewed. Never mind that the book was entitled *A Pictorial Guide to Domestic Sanitary Defects.*[10] It was leather-bound; it had to be an antique.

---

[10] Yes, it is a real book. The full title is *Dangers to Health: A Pictorial Guide to Domestic Sanitary Defects* by the wonderfully named T. Pridgin Teale (London: J. & A. Churchill, 1878). Order it from your library now!

Just because something looks old doesn't mean it's an antique. Similarly, just because something sounds biblical, that doesn't make it holy.

I read a lot of songs in preparing this book and what was noticeable was what I called Lamb Quotient or LQ. These are songs which use images such as 'the Lamb', 'Zion' or 'banners', or words like 'magnify'. Even though these songs might not be directly quoting the Bible, they still retreat into biblical imagery and quasi-biblical language.

Songs of Fellowship has, for example, a high Lamb Quotient. You can't move in that book without tripping over a lamb or without some songwriter waving a banner in your face. *Spring Harvest 2003* has a pretty high LQ, but that's partly because it contains well-known songs from previous years as well as new stuff. The Soul Survivor collections have a fairly low LQ, although even they have sprinklings of lambs, fortresses, swords and even the odd tabernacle.

Even when worship songs do not rip words straight from the Bible, they use the same imagery. You don't have to quote the Bible, you can just use stuff that *sounds* like the Bible! I have found songs which include references to 'entering the sanctuary', songs which talk about 'ministering to the holy throne'. Such lines might have come from 1850, or 1700, or 1610 or even 1000 BC. But to find them in songs written in 2002 – and songs mainly aimed at young people – is astonishing. It would be interesting to read this to members of a congregation and ask them what it meant.

Our worship songs are full of images from thousands of years ago, often expressed in a kind of Ye Olde Holy Bible English. The result is songs that sound like the Authorised Version of the Bible as rewritten by J.R.R. Tolkein. You get songs which talk about the morning star, an image which meant something when people got up at dawn. But now? Now, we all use alarm clocks.

Using well-worn, not to say worn-out, images is more lazy writing. Finding new pictures is hard, far easier just to take an old one out of the box and click it into place. Finding new pictures requires artistry and imagination; using old images just requires the ability to follow the crowd. Which may be the point. Because the fact is that many Christians – especially in the evangelical church – distrust art. Art, by its very nature, involves an artist; it involves a personal interpretation or expression. Many churches don't feel comfortable with that idea, even though it happens every week in the sermon. They'd rather hear statements of doctrine than an individual's ideas; they'd rather hear dogma than personal reflection; they'd rather have images from the Bible than images from an individual's imagination.

In this context, worship song writers are always slightly on the defensive. Although from the very start hymns and worship songs have been personal works of art, in a culture that distrusts art, any song which is perceived as too 'creative' is vulnerable. In a culture where Scripture is acceptable but art distrusted, the easiest thing for the artist is to make his art sound like Scripture. Then we're all happy.

The problem is that it results in songs full of imagery which have no relevance and meaning for the contemporary Christian. Jesus talked about shepherds not merely because of Israel's historic links with sheep farmers, but because everyone in his audience knew a shepherd. Many, indeed, were shepherds. So the metaphor had both potency and immediacy.

Not so today. Singing 'you are the shepherd, we are the sheep' may well have a biblical precedent, but to a modern, urban congregation it's almost meaningless.

Most of them wouldn't know a shepherd if one came up and belted them over the head with his crook. And the only sheep they see is hanging in bits in the supermarket meat department.

These are no longer images with a power to strike to the heart; they are code words which have to be deciphered. Worship songs grow to resemble crossword puzzles, where only those who know the phraseology can decipher the clues. It's like the biblical version of cockney rhyming slang. Now this is all very well, but the point about codes is that you have to know the code in order to crack it. And most people today don't know the code. So, to help, why not photocopy the following and pin it up in church. Or whack it up on PowerPoint during your singing.

Nick's Worship-Speak Phrasebook

Confused about what the images mean? Just use this handy guide and you'll be speaking like someone from the seventeenth century in no time!

silver and gold =	riches, wealth
Lamb =	Jesus
Lamb of God =	Jesus again
Lamb who was slain =	that'll be Jesus again
blood of the Lamb =	salvation
risen Lamb =	guess who?
refining/refiner's fire =	making me pure
sheep =	us
Shepherd =	Jesus again
Morning star =	er ... that'll be Jesus probably
every tribe and nation =	all the people on earth
Bridegroom =	Jesus
bride =	the church

harvest	=	judgement and/or evangelism
trumpets, harps, psaltery	=	general musical instruments
mountains	=	the biggest things in the world
vineyard	=	no idea. Probably Jesus

Sometimes this over-use of biblical images actually takes us away from what they meant in the Bible.

Let's take the image of 'refining'. I've lost count of the number of songs that use the metaphor of 'refining' or 'refiner's fire' or 'refined like silver or gold'. The number of times that it's used leads me to suspect that there is some kind of huge smelting subculture in the Christian church that I was previously unaware of. Apparently, completely unknown to me, my fellow Christians rush home from the services and start heating various slabs of metal in enormous crucibles.

I would challenge any reader of this book to ask a member of their congregation or a young person in their youth group what 'refiner's fire' means. I'm not sure that any of them could correctly identify what happens during the refining process, but still we trot out this tired old metaphor. It's so much easier to use the code word than it is to think of a new metaphor for being purified. After all, refining sounds so posh, doesn't it? It sounds so scriptural.

And it's not as if there aren't other images of purifying around. Even the Bible uses other metaphors. Malachi uses a very simple image along with 'refining':

> On the day the Lord comes, he will be like a furnace that purifies silver or like strong soap in a washbasin. No one will be able to stand up to him.
>
> (Mal. 3:2, CEV)

There aren't many songs which talk of us being washed with 'strong soap'. If we're washed at all, we're generally 'cleansed with hyssop'. But the point here is more than just the use of an old image. This verse also points to a way in which, I think, 'refining' has actually changed its meaning. In the Bible, talk of God as 'refining' or as a 'refiner' is generally used to describe the suffering that we go through that makes us better followers of God.[11]

> I tested you in hard times just as silver is refined in a heated furnace.
>
> (Is. 48:10, CEV)

1 Peter talks about our faith being refined as we 'suffer grief in all kinds of trials' (1 Pet. 1:6, NIV). It's not a *pleasant* process. It's not something that the followers of God, whether in the Old Testament or New, wholeheartedly wished for. They would have understood what we often forget: that if something is refined it has to endure enormous heat. And the heat is key to the understanding of the image. The Bible generally uses the term to help people understand why they were suffering. 'Yes, you are undergoing enormous suffering and trial,' says Peter to the persecuted church, 'but it will purify you; it will make you holy.' The songs which use the refining metaphor tend to forget about the suffering bit. They're very happy about the 'purifying' and 'making holy' bit. But when most Christians sing 'refiner's fire' I'm sure they're not asking God to give them a bit more suffering in their life.

It's not like we're short, in our hygiene obsessed society, of alternative images. Most homes have washing machines or baths or showers; there's the car wash or the high-pressure hose; people drink filtered water. Admittedly the

---

[11] See Ps. 66:10, 11; Is. 48:10; Jer. 9:7; 1 Pet. 1:6, 7.

refining image has the advantage of both purifying and making more valuable; pure metal is more valuable than its unrefined version. But I'm not sure people recognise these kinds of references. I suspect most people might think of a petrol refinery, and that conjures up images of smoke, pollution and greenhouse gases.

Other images that come to mind that you might use, in place of the ubiquitous furnace include:

- the way in which the sea washes a stone smooth
- the way in which sandpaper smooths away rough wood
- the polishing of stones, steps worn smooth by time
- furniture polished
- floors scrubbed clean
- clothes spun and dried
- rusted metal cleaned away by sand-blasting …

You see? It's not so hard to come up with other ideas. Shaping them into a song, though, *is* hard work. It requires discipline and creativity and perseverance. Making the image fit, making it appropriate and right, that's not easy. I agree; it's far easier to stick with refining fire. Even if there isn't much smelting going on in your church.

Sometimes, indeed, words we think are scriptural aren't actually found in Scripture at all. The word 'Jehovah', for example, which features in so many songs, isn't found in the Bible. It's an invention dating from the Middle Ages, when a monk combined the Hebrew initials used in YHWH with the vowels from the word Adonai, meaning the Lord … well, it gets complicated.

But 'Jehovah' doesn't appear in the Bible. And anyway, the names of God that we sing of in our songs – names like *Jehovah-jireh* or *Jehovah-nissi* – aren't actually names of God, but names of places or commemorations of events (see Gen. 22:14; Ex. 17:15). Jehovah is another code word. Sounds old, must be biblical.

So far we've been looking at Bible images. To some extent I can forgive their repeated use, although, as I've shown, it would be better to use more potent, modern images where possible.

What is harder to excuse are the sheer number of 'biblical' verbs that make their way into our songs. It's one thing to insist on using the image of the Lamb in your songs; it does, at least, crop up quite a lot in the Bible. But it's another thing to use words like 'magnify' and 'exalt'. These aren't Bible images, they're sixteenth-century verbs; their origin lies not in the Hebrew Scriptures but in the King James version.

How many people today understand what the word 'magnify' means as it is used in worship songs? 'Magnify' today means to make something very small appear very large. So when we magnify God it sounds to a modern ear like God is a microbe under the microscope. 'Magnify' in the King James version, or in old hymns, means 'to glorify'; to 'praise, or give honour to'. And, interestingly, the OED lists it as an 'archaic' word.

Modern songs are peppered with these archaic words. These are not Bible themes – such as grace or redemption or salvation; or even Bible images such as shepherds, vineyards and lambs; they're just old-fashioned words, which, because they are associated with God, have somehow been sanctified. They are words with haloes round them, glowing in the light of spirituality.

A rough checklist of these words would include the following:

Verbs

- Exalt
- Magnify
- Anoint
- Seek
- Extol
- Bless (as in 'bless your name')
- Minister

Nouns

- Fortress
- Tower
- Burden
- Robe
- Garment
- Canopy
- Gates
- Captives

The only reason I can see for using any of these words is to make your song sound more holy. They all have perfectly usable modern equivalents. So why not use them?

Worship songs aren't ancient texts, they are the children of our culture and time. So why clothe them in antique costume? I'd rather have a modern painting than a copy of an Old Master. I'd rather have genuine new furniture than reproductions.

It's modern: it can't be holy

The flip side of using archaic language and imagery is that songwriters don't use modern images. If you don't believe me, try looking through whatever collection of worship songs you use and find a modern image, an image that, say, could only have come from the twentieth century.

Here's what I found.

Collection	Total songs	Songs using modern images
Songs of Fellowship	640	3
Spring Harvest	150	4
Soul Survivor and Update	300	7

So there we have it. Out of some 1,000 songs, only fourteen use any distinctive, contemporary image. You can find flocks of lambs, vats of anointing oil, enough two-edged swords and chariots to stock an army. But no cars. No electricity. No Internet, newspapers or TV. No trains. (Well, I did find one train, but only in a song which talked about God's train filling the temple. The song, written in 1999, seems to have been written for young people. I wonder how many of them stood there imagining God arriving on the 3.15 from Paddington?)[12]

Three of the 'modern' songs listed above were written for children, one of the few areas of worship where modern images abound. Children, you see, can't be expected to understand biblical imagery, so we use telephones and butterflies and express trains. It's not their fault, poor dears. They'll grow up soon enough and then they can start singing about really relevant images like ... um ... castles and strongholds and all that.

Why is it that we're afraid of the modern world? Perhaps it's because, both as congregations and artists, we don't appreciate how much God is a part of the modern world. But God is here, all around us, intimately involved in our

---

[12] It was probably going to Bristol Temple Meads.

daily lives. I do not believe in a God who is remote from the ordinary world. I believe in a God who knows about beer as well as wine, who might actually prefer to wash me with soap, rather than cleanse me with hyssop.

Perhaps it's simply a failure of technique. There is no doubt that finding and using modern images for worship songs is a difficult task. But I would suggest that it's only difficult because everyone avoids it. The more people who try, the more who work at it, the easier and more natural it will be. It is the role of the artist to challenge the present, not recreate the past.

Dare to be different

Perhaps it's that the writers want to use modern images, but are scared to do so, for fear of being thought foolish. Well, the answer is to write what you have to, not what you think the audience wants to hear. Prophecy – the speaking of truth – should not be imprisoned by the expectations of the audience.

The sad fact is that if you use modern language you may well get ridiculed. There are those who cannot look beyond the words to the images; to them a song is not holy unless it's couched in holy language.

Indeed, some of the responses to the original article I wrote on this subject condemned me for wanting to fill every song with ordinary images. Well, here's a fact: we live in an ordinary world. We have a God who is interested in ordinary life. I don't worship a God for whom I have to use a special language. Jesus came as a man into our world. He came as a *tekton*, a carpenter, a sort of odd-job man. He worked in a small, ordinary town for most of his life. God likes ordinary people; he just wants to make them extraordinary. He likes transforming water into wine. He uses ordinary images to describe himself; images of sheep and gates and bread and wine. He likes taking ordinary images as a way into people's hearts. I don't want worship songs to become prosaic and dull. I want to see everyday images transformed by the imaginations of our worship song writers in order to lead us into a new understanding of God.

Of course it's not easy. And people will get it wrong. But even when it doesn't come out perfect, it can still have enormous power. Willard Sperry tells the following story:

> There is, for example, painted on a wall behind the pulpit in a little Baptist church in a fishing village down on the coast of Maine, a ship's anchor. It is the only attempt at religious symbolism in an otherwise bare meeting house. The anchor itself is not perfect as a work of art. The painter has wrestled rather ineffectually with the problem of perspective and the three dimensions. But for all its queer flat angularity it is one of the best pieces of chancel art I know, simply because it suggests what the Christian religion means to those who go down to the sea in ships.[13]

The strength of this image lay not in its execution, which was obviously a bit rough and ready; the strength lay in the fact that the metaphor was taken from the world of the people to whom it was addressed. They knew what an anchor was and what it did; and they saw in that a powerful, potent message about God.

Worship songs and hymns are the poetry of the ordinary believer. They're a route into people's hearts. And to get there fastest and most securely, we have to use images that people know. How are people supposed to grasp who Jesus really is if we're always making him sound like a

---

[13] Willard Sperry, *Reality in Worship*, p. 215.

character from Shakespeare? How are they supposed to know that God loves them here and now if we're always talking about him in the language of yesterday? How are we supposed to get across that our God is interested in ordinary people, if we're always using words and images they don't understand?

The problem with using images like the code words we talked about is that people feel excluded. I talked at the beginning of this book about the non-Christians in Luton who could not make head or tail of the lyrics. But the truth is that there are hundreds of thousands of Christians in the pews and seats of our churches who haven't got a clue what the code words mean either. They don't read their Bibles, or the Bibles they read might not be the kind that contain those sorts of images. Now we can moan about that, we can take the moral high-ground and argue that all Christians should read their Bibles. But at the same time we have to accept that they don't all read their Bibles. And even those who do forget a lot of what they read. That means that we have to work from both directions; both encouraging people to read the Scriptures, but not denying them access to worship if they don't. By all means encourage people to read their Bibles in the future, but don't make it impossible for them to understand the songs here and now.

It's not an impossible task. In researching this book I was heartened by indications that worship song writers themselves are identifying the need. Matt Redman writes,

> I'm realising more and more that as worship leaders we need to widen our 'song vocabulary' to included songs for every biblical theme and every walk of life.[14]

---

[14] Matt Redman (ed.), *Heart of Worship Files*, p. 41.

While Paul Oakley writes,

> Sometimes the simple ideas are the best. The biggest challenge is to find a fresh way to express ancient truths that have already been written about for hundreds of years and to find fresh ways to respond to and apply those things.[15]

Several songwriters, it seems to me, are making an effort to craft simple, accessible, but high-impact lyrics. Kendrick is one of the few writers with the stature and the ability to deliver these kind of knock-out punches. Nor is he afraid to confront modern issues. His song 'Beauty for Brokenness' deals with a great many modern issues and ills from despair to wars, from unemployment to environmental degradation. This is a song about real life and about our commitment to others.

Perhaps the most successful exponents of the consciously modern worship song have been the Iona songs developed by John L. Bell. Bell's approach to worship song writing was informed by the time he spent working in inner-city Glasgow. He developed a communal approach to song writing, in order to find a way of allowing unchurched young people to express their faith. Bell and his collaborator Graham Maule also drew on world music. They founded the Wild Goose Worship Group which included in its founder members teenagers, some of whom were unemployed and many of whom came from an unchurched background.

The language in their songs is more robust and earthy; perhaps sometimes more everyday than we are used to. They are simple without being trite, and they draw heavily on songs from other cultures for their inspiration, as well as from Scotland's native folk-song tradition. Their hymns

---

[15] Matt Redman (ed.), *Heart of Worship Files*, p. 152.

talk about difficult issues and real human emotions. And they're not afraid to use ordinary language and images. 'Christ's is the world' includes lines such as:

> Feel for the parents who've lost their child,
> Feel for the women whom men have defiled,
> Feel for the baby for whom there's no breast,
> And feel for the weary who find no rest.[16]

These are powerful images. They involve us in the modern world, because they come from our world. No sheep. No two-edged swords. Just hungry, desperate people in need of God's love.

Many people do not like anything 'modern'. 'For many people, living dangerously is a frightening experience.'[17] They'll take comfort in familiar words, metaphors and images. It's not that the pictures taken straight out of the Bible mean very much to them any more, it's just that they're so, well, comforting.

The strange thing is that, although the people who feel this way about worship songs would hate to be bracketed with the church traditionalists, that's exactly who they resemble. Just as certain parts of the traditionalist wing of the church wants to keep the King James Bible and the 1662 Prayer Book because 'the language is so poetic', a lot of modern traditionalists want to keep the same old vocabulary in use in their worship songs. These people wouldn't speak that way and wouldn't want their preachers to use the same antiquated language, but they don't want to have songs in a modern language. They are traditionalists; they're just being traditional about a different form of worship.

---

[16] John L. Bell and Graham Maule, 'Christ's is the world', SOF 685, 1989 (Permission granted for use.).

[17] Andrew Wilson-Dickson, *A Brief History of Christian Music*, p. 411.

Koine worship

We worship a non-traditional God. We worship a God who is always doing something new and who always wants to communicate to ordinary people in their language.

Perhaps the best example of this is the New Testament itself. For many years, New Testament scholars were rather embarrassed by the New Testament because the Greek in which it was written was so inelegant and rough. Compared to the great philosophers, the New Testament writers were rough and ready scribblers. They called it 'degenerate attic', which means degenerate Greek.

Then archaeologists discovered a huge cache of Greek 'trade' documents; orders, receipts, letters written by ordinary tradesmen and businessmen to their colleagues and clients. And the thing about these documents was that they were all written in the same kind of Greek that the New Testament was written in. This was called koine Greek – ordinary Greek. Koine means 'common'.

The implications of this are, I believe, profound. It means that the New Testament was not written in 'holy' language. It was not even written in the genteel, philosophical, academic language of the ancient philosophers. It was written in the common language of ordinary people, using images and vocabulary that they could understand. Christianity is not a faith which can only be understood and appreciated by academics or experts or philosophers or refined, artistic types. It's for ordinary people. And they need to hear it in a language they understand.

Just as the New Testament writers chose to write in common Greek, we need koine songwriters who write koine songs; songs of the people for the people. The experts might call them 'degenerate', but that doesn't matter – because the ordinary people will understand.

Key points

- Just because it's in the Bible doesn't mean it's going to make a great lyric.

- We should keep the amount of 'biblical' language down to a minimum.

- Where possible try to find new images that have a contemporary relevance.

- Run the risk: try to keep your language and your images modern and simple.

- Don't just quote the Bible, explore and explain it.

Key questions

- Do you just cut and paste Bible references into your songs?

- Do you use Bible-type language to make your songs sound more spiritual?

- Look around you. Look at the world you live in. What are the common objects, the well-known pictures in people's lives?

- Examine the work of great contemporary songwriters and poets. What images do they use? Can you do the same?

- Are there everyday objects that can be used as metaphors for God's kingdom?

- If you want to use a Bible metaphor can you break it down to see what it is saying? Is there a modern metaphor that could do the job?

- Do you consciously store up metaphors and pictures? Do you keep a log book of ideas?

Kevin Molecule
27a Cinderpile Crescent
Stoke Poges

Mr Dave Davey
Songs of Dwellingness Ministries
Briglimpton
SUSSEX

Hi Dave,

You know I'm really coming to terms with what
being a worship leader means. The role of
a worship leader is to lead, isn't it? And
leadership means that people follow you; not
the other way round.

See, sometimes, people can't follow you
where you're going. That's what Josh said
to me the other day when I was taking him
through my new set of lyrics. 'Kev,' he said,
'I don't quite follow you.'

'No, Josh,' I said, and I think there was a
sadness in my voice. 'I don't think you do.'

Not sure if he got the point I was trying
to make. But then again, he is a drummer.
Let's never forget that.

I'm trying to take them with me, you see.
Trying to take them on my artistic journey.
But they're so unspiritual. I don't think
I'll talk my lyrics through with them any
more. I think it's better for them to work
at what I'm trying to say, right? You know,
figure it out for themselves.

That's what's really behind my latest
lyric. It's a challenging work, I admit. But

people have to work at worship, don't they.
I don't want to spoon-feed them or anything
like that.

Benaiah-like I face the snowy lions, oh God[1]
Stepping in the sand-marks where you trod,[2]
I don't care if it makes me odd,[3]
I want to hunt like Nimrod,[4]
In Gaza, Gath and Ashdod[5]
Where Dagon falls right down on the floor
   before my God[6]
Don't let me be like Ichabod[7]
And don't let me be like King Herod[8]
But in my old clothes, washed in the blood,[9]
I want to stand where you have stod.[10]

Chorus
Oh Lord, don't let us miss the appointment,
When we receive your big anointment.[11]

This is a personal statement, I know. But
I feel it has integrity. I suppose it is
true that to fully understand it you have
to know a lot of the Bible and also to spot
various references to my own life. Actually,
I suppose to fully understand it you have
to be me. But surely if being a leader means
anything, it means wanting people to follow
in your footsteps.

   And, from now on, if people want to follow
me, they'll have to move church. Because the
time has come for me to move on from the Stoke
Poges Strict Tabernacle. I've been offered
the post of worship leader at the Stoke Poges
Relaxed Tabernacle, which, frankly, is a more
fun place to be.

Thanks for all your encouragement, and for your unquestioning acceptance of my anointed work. The fact that you have never commented on my songs or altered a word has taught me a lot.

With deep heat,

Kevin Molecule
Worship Leader

P.S. In order to help you grasp my anointing, I've added these references to explain the song words.

[1] See 2 Sam. 23:20, 21.
[2] This refers to a vision I had of a child walking along sand and trying to step in the footsteps of their father. When I told Josh about it, he said, why didn't I put the whole thing in instead of just referring to him. Honestly! Not an ounce of spiritual poetry in his body.
[3] This refers to what some kids in the street called me the other day. Well, actually they didn't say 'odd', but I thought putting in 'completely bonkers, mate' would ruin the rhyme scheme.
[4] See Gen. 10:8, 9. Nimrod hunted with the 'strength of the LORD'. So what I'm saying here is that I want the Lord's strength.
[5] See Josh. 11:22. These were Philistine towns, i.e. enemy territory. So put this together with the previous line and I'm saying 'I want the strength to fight the enemy.' But it's so much more deep this way, I think.
[6] See 1 Sam. 5:5. You have to sing these words a bit quickly otherwise the melody goes all wrong, but I think they are all necessary.
[7] See 1 Sam. 4:21. Ichabod means 'no glory'.
[8] See Mt. 2.1, 3, 4, 7, 12, 13, 15, 16, 19; 14:1, 3-6; Mk. 6:14, 16, 17, 20-22, 25; 8:15; Lk. 1:5; 3: 1, 19, 20; 9:7, 9; 13:31; 23:7-9, 11, 12, 15; Acts 4:27; 12:1, 3, 4, 11, 19-21, 23.

[9] You have to pronounce this as 'blod' otherwise it just doesn't rhyme.

[10] Josh says this isn't a word. But it sounds OK to me.

[11] This refers to me missing a dentist appointment the other day and I thought 'Gosh, what if I missed an appointment with God?'

Conclusion: or
Where do we go from here?

The poetry of the heart

I wrote this book because I think that worship songs are important.

Critics have always looked down on the songs that church congregations have sung. There has been a snobbery at work; a view that hymns – and latterly worship songs – might be OK for those who don't know any better, but they're really just second-rate poetry for people who cannot cope with the real thing.

It is true that many hymns and worship songs – a great many hymns and worship songs – are second-rate poems. (Some of them, to be honest, dream of being that good!) But some of them, I believe, are first-rate poems. It's just they're not the kind of poetry that posh people enjoy. As George Sampson wrote,

> The hymn has been the poor man's poetry, the only poetry that has ever come home to his heart.[1]

This is one of the key facts that we have to grasp: people will remember what they sing. Hymns and worship songs have a way of sticking in the memory when far

---

[1] G. Sampson, 'Century of Divine Songs' in *Proceedings of the British Academy*, 29 (1943) 37–64, p. 37.

grander verse fades away. Even someone like D.H. Lawrence couldn't escape the memory of the songs he had sung.

> ... all these lovely poems woven deep into a man's consciousness are still not woven so deep in me as the rather banal Nonconformist hymns that penetrated through and through my childhood.[2]

The truth is that, done right, hymns and worship songs touch people's hearts. This is beyond the emotional pull that I talked of earlier, it's something far deeper. Make the words right and they will write themselves on people's hearts. Make the words right and they will form part of people's lives. Make the words right and they will open people's eyes to the reality of God. Make the words right and, as they sing them, God will come home to people's hearts.

Ten commandments

So how do we do that? One of the things we have to do is address our technique; how we put the songs together. The words, the structures, the tools that we use to help people respond to God in worship.

In a famous essay, 'Politics and the English Language',[3] George Orwell proposed a set of rules or guidelines for anyone wanting to write clear, distinctive, simple English prose. I think what we need is a similar set of guidelines. I'm not conceited enough to compare myself to Orwell, nor to claim that I should be the arbiter of what's acceptable in

[2] D.H. Lawrence, 'Hymns in a Man's Life' in *Selected Literary Criticism*, A. Beal (ed.) (London: Heinemann, 1956), p. 6.
[3] George Orwell, *Selected Essays* (London: Penguin Books, 1957), pp. 143–57.

worship songs. I'd merely like to suggest some approaches which, if nothing else, might help today's worship song writers in their work. You may agree with these, you may disagree; but I hope you will take the opportunity to write your own rules, to list your own values that will define and inform your writing.

1. *Take it seriously*

   It is a great responsibility to pass on a message from God; make sure you get it right. Precision matters. The angels are watching your punctuation.

2. *Work hard at your craft*

   Practise, practise, practise. Refuse to be satisfied. Always try to climb higher. Never say 'that'll do'.

3. *Make every word count*

   Be prepared to justify every single word you use. Avoid repetition. Pursue simplicity. Brevity is next to godliness.

4. *Test your words*

   Try your words on others. Test them to destruction. Then put them back together, only stronger than before.

5. *Share the load*

   Work with lyricists and poets as well as preachers and teachers. Seek out and encourage their development in churches. Find people who love words and get them to talk about God.

6. *Never stop learning*

   Read great poetry, great song lyrics, the works of great hymn writers. Learn, don't copy. Give what you learn new shape in your own work.

7. *Don't use old words if new ones are as good*

   Some words have no substitute. But where there is a modern alternative, use it. Our day-to-day language can be holy.

8. *Find new images*

   Reject worn-out images and pictures. Don't use it 'just because it's in the Bible'. Find pictures that strike the heart; pictures that make people look with new eyes.

9. *Tell me about God*

   Avoid introspection and self-obsession. Worship is a response to God. Someday you will be gone. Your words will live on, if they focus on someone who was, and is, and will be for ever.

10. *Go deeper*

    Deep songs spring from deep experiences. Contemplation counts. Walk your own path with God and bring us all something back.

The servant-lyric

Worship songs matter. Earlier, I talked about worship leaders as servants. The same is surely true of worship song lyrics.

The words should serve those singing them. Our words should explain, reveal, inspire – even occasionally startle – but they should only do so as a means of helping people into worship. They are not for showing off rich vocabulary or technical virtuosity or even how many Scriptures the writer has read. They are servant-lyrics, aiming to serve the church by leading it into greater understanding, truth and worship.

This idea, of a lyric that is the servant of its audience, is not a fashionable one. We are in an artistic culture which promotes the 'master-lyric'. Much modern art and culture is deliberately confusing, opaque or subjective, expressed in a language that only the artist truly understands. And if we the public don't understand that particular poem, painting or sculpture, well, then that's our fault. We're just not artistic enough.

We must not allow this attitude to seep into the worship song. I have said that all hymns and worship songs have an element of the subjective about them; they are borne out of the writer's personal experience with God. But they cannot *only* be about that. And they cannot be couched in a language that only the lyric writer understands. The subjective lyric cannot serve the church; we are inviting people to share in worship, not spend time trying to decipher our inmost thoughts and emotions.

Instead we need servant-lyrics. We need writers who constantly ask, 'How can I serve the church with this song? How can I express what I know of God in a way that will help others?'

What makes a servant-lyric?

1. The servant-lyric does not confuse its audience by using language that they do not understand, or images that are so worn out as to be practically useless. It seeks to find new ways to express timeless truths; new images to bring the reality of God into the lives of those who are worshipping.

2. The servant-lyric does not try to show off or be clever; it's not a display of technique for the sake of technique. It has technique; indeed, it's the product of good technique; but it's not just an exercise in rhyming or verse structure.

3. The servant-lyric is simple and comprehensible; it is a road into worship and understanding. Servant-lyrics are not poetry; they are designed to be sung and to be understood.

4. A servant-lyric is real. It connects with real life and allows people to identify with its subject matter. Sperry says the minister should ask the following questions:

   > Is what we have now before us real? Is it true in itself? Is it true for us? Is there anything in our own lives as Christians to which it corresponds, and which it helps us to say out, simply and directly to God and to each other?[4]

5. The servant-lyric encourages people to go deeper. In C.S. Lewis's book *The Last Battle*,[5] he gives a picture of heaven in which there is always more to be discovered, always more to see. Great worship songs – and I believe this is something that cannot be manufactured but comes as a gift from God – have this ability. They offer an ocean of possi-bilities; we can paddle at the water's edge, swim out in the shallows, or dive deep into the depths. But, at whatever level, there are *always discoveries to be made.*

A lyric with these qualities can only come as a gift from God – or rather as a combination of gifts from God. It is God's grace, working with the craftsmanship and artistry of the writer. It cannot be manufactured. But we know it when we see it. And the songs that have this quality are the songs that last.

---

[4] Willard Sperry, *Reality in Worship*, p. 211.
[5] C.S. Lewis, *The Last Battle*, first published 1956 by The Bodley Head Ltd.

Appendix 1:
Some technical stuff

Rhyme scheme

The rhyme scheme is merely a way of showing how a particular poem rhymes. It uses a simple a, b, c format to identify each rhyme.

So, a verse from Wesley's 'And can it be'[1] has a rhyme scheme that can be described as a b a b c c c c. Here's how it works.

'Tis mystery all: th' Immortal dies!	a
Who can explore his strange design?	b
In vain the firstborn seraph tries	a
to sound the depths of love divine.	b
'Tis mercy all! Let earth adore;	c
let angel minds inquire no more.	c
'Tis mercy all! Let earth adore;	c
let angel minds inquire no more.	c

Metre

The metre of a poem or hymn is a way of describing the line length by counting the number of syllables.

So, a line like 'Praise God from whom all blessings flow'[2] has eight syllables:

---

[1] Charles Wesley, 1707–88.
[2] Words by Thomas Ken (1674), *Baptist Hymnal*, no. 766.

1	2	3	4	5	6 7	8

Praise God from whom all blessings flow

In hymns the layout of a verse can be indicated numerically. For example, to continue with the hymn above:

> Praise God from whom all blessings flow,
> Praise Him, all creatures here below,
> Praise Him above, ye heavenly host;
> Praise Father, Son and Holy Ghost.

This verse has four lines, each with eight syllables. In some hymn books you will see this represented as 8.8.8.8.

The most common metrical arrangements of hymns are:

Long metre

Four lines of 8 syllables (8.8.8.8)

Common metre

Alternate lines of 8 and 6 syllables (8.6.8.6)

Short metre

Three lines of 6 and one of 8 syllables (6.6.8.6)

Appendix 2:
Literary patterns

Many hymns and worship songs use structural techniques to give a unity to their thought and argument.

Narrative

Many hymns and songs tell a narrative through their story. Many of these, such as Graham Kendrick's 'Led like a lamb to the slaughter' or Crossman's 'My Song is Love Unknown', tell the story of the passion; others tell a kind of story of individual salvation and experience, such as Newton's 'Amazing Grace' (see above, p. 71). Even a song such as 'When the music fades' tells a story – in this case the story of an individual coming to a personal realisation of what worship means.[3] Virtually all Christmas carols are narratives.

Itemisation

This looks at one theme, but each time from a different angle.

For example, the hymn 'Breathe on me, breath of God', written by Edwin Hatch,[4] begins each verse with a development of the main theme.

---

[3] Matt Redman, 'When the music fades', SOF 1113, 1997.
[4] Died 1889.

1. Breathe on me, breath of God
   Fill me with life anew …

2. Breathe on me, breath of God
   Until my heart is pure …

3. Breathe on me, breath of God
   Till I am wholly thine …

4. Breathe on me, breath of God
   So I shall never die …

A modern song like 'Your will, not mine' uses the same technique.[5]

Questions

A lot of hymns use rhetorical questions to open up a kind of dialogue with those singing:

> And can it be that I should gain
> An interest in the saviour's blood?

Or Crossman's[6] 'My Song is Love Unknown' which ends the first verse with:

> O who am I, that for my sake,
> My Lord should take frail flesh and die?

Call and response

This is a pattern that has grown out of folk song and spirituals (see 'Oh, my Lord!' on p. 13 for another example).

It consists of a first statement and then a response or tag line. Frequently the lines are split between men and

---

[5] Dougie Brown, 'Your will, not mine', SOF 1149, 1991.
[6] Samuel Crossman, 1624–83.

women. The most common model is that the men give the call and the women respond. Whether this is based out of a male-centric theology I wouldn't like to say.

Appendix 3:
Kevin's songs

Kevin's songs are based on real lines from real worship songs. He won't thank me for telling you that, but it's true. Obviously he has brought his own anointing to bear on them; he's expanded them, developed them, occasionally ruined them; but apart from lines which are obviously his (such as the Benaiah one) he's drawn heavily on modern worship language. The fact is that there is little in Kevin's work that you will not find in the latest worship books.

Kevin's new CD, *The man who put the 'hip' in 'worship'*, is currently available on Songs of Dwellingness Records.

Kevin has recently left the Stoke Poges Relaxed Tabernacle and is currently Worship-Prophet at Stoke Poges Far Out Tabernacle. He is a regular worship leader at Spring Bounce, Blackbelt and the Soul Revolver festivals.